I0446169

Introduction: Embarking on the VBA Odyssey

Briefly introduce the power of VBA in accounting

Visual Basic for Applications (VBA) is a powerful scripting language developed by Microsoft, primarily used for automation and customization of tasks in Microsoft Office applications, including Excel. In the context of accounting, VBA can be a game-changer, offering several key benefits:

1. Automation of repetitive tasks: VBA allows accountants to automate repetitive and time-consuming tasks, such as data entry, calculations, and report generation. This frees up valuable time for accountants to focus on more strategic and analytical aspects of their work.

2. Enhanced accuracy: By using VBA to automate calculations and data processing, the risk of manual errors is significantly reduced. This is particularly critical in accounting, where precision and accuracy are paramount for financial integrity.

3. Customization for unique workflows: VBA provides the flexibility to create customized solutions tailored to specific accounting workflows. Accountants can design scripts to match the unique requirements of their organization, ensuring a more efficient and personalized approach to tasks.

4. Streamlined reporting: VBA can be applied to streamline the creation of financial reports. Automation of reporting processes ensures consistency, reduces the likelihood of errors, and allows for quick adjustments to changing reporting needs.

5. Efficient data analysis: VBA can extend the capabilities of Excel for data analysis in accounting. It enables the creation of sophisticated algorithms and analytical tools, empowering accountants to derive meaningful insights from financial data.

6. Scalability and productivity: As accountants become more proficient in VBA, they can scale their automation efforts to handle larger datasets and more complex tasks. This scalability leads to increased productivity and efficiency in accounting workflows.

In summary, the power of VBA in accounting lies in its ability to automate, customize, and streamline various processes. By harnessing the capabilities of VBA, accountants can elevate their efficiency, reduce errors, and spend more time on strategic financial analysis and decision-making.

The potential for automation in enhancing productivity

The potential for automation in enhancing productivity using VBA in accounting is immense, offering a transformative impact on traditional accounting workflows. Here are key highlights:

1. Time savings: VBA automation drastically reduces the time spent on repetitive and manual tasks, such as data entry, calculations, and report generation. Accountants can redirect their efforts toward more strategic and value-added activities.

2. Consistency and accuracy: Automation through VBA ensures a high level of consistency and accuracy in accounting processes. By eliminating the risk of manual errors, financial data becomes more reliable, enhancing the overall integrity of financial reports.

3. Efficient data handling: VBA enables the efficient handling and manipulation of large datasets. Accountants can process vast amounts of financial information quickly and accurately, facilitating timely decision-making and analysis.

4. Customization for specific needs: VBA allows accountants to tailor automation scripts to meet the unique requirements of their organization. Whether it's creating custom reports or automating industry-specific calculations, VBA provides the flexibility needed for a personalized approach.

5. Streamlined reporting: Automation using VBA streamlines the reporting process, ensuring that financial reports are generated consistently and promptly. This is particularly beneficial for month-end and year-end reporting, where time is often a critical factor.

6. Adaptability to changing requirements: VBA scripts can be easily adapted to accommodate changes in accounting procedures or reporting standards. This adaptability ensures that the automation remains relevant and effective in the face of evolving business needs.

7. Increased productivity and workload handling: With routine tasks automated, accountants can handle higher workloads without sacrificing accuracy or quality. This scalability allows accounting teams to manage more extensive datasets and complex financial analyses efficiently.

8. Empowering non-programmers: VBA provides a user-friendly scripting language, making automation accessible to accountants without extensive programming backgrounds. This empowers finance professionals to take control of their automation needs and reduces reliance on external resources.

In essence, VBA automation in accounting is a catalyst for increased productivity, allowing accountants to focus on strategic decision-making, analysis, and adding significant value to their organizations. The time and resource savings achieved through VBA automation contribute directly to a more efficient and effective accounting function.

The exciting journey ahead

Embark on a thrilling journey into the future of accounting—a journey where mundane tasks transform into moments of creative brilliance, and every spreadsheet becomes a canvas for innovation. In "Automate to Elevate: VBA Secrets for Accountants," the adventure begins with the click of a button and the power of Visual Basic for Applications (VBA).

Picture a world where your daily accounting routine is no longer a chore but a symphony of automated precision. Imagine unlocking the hidden potential of Excel, turning complex calculations into elegant scripts, and tailoring every report to perfection. This isn't just a book; it's your passport to a realm where productivity knows no bounds.

As you flip through the pages, discover the art of scripting, the dance of data, and the magic of personalized automation. Each chapter unveils a new dimension of VBA, empowering you to reshape the way you work. From the fundamentals to advanced customization, this journey is designed for accounting wizards ready to redefine efficiency.

Are you prepared to break free from the shackles of manual tasks and embrace a world where errors are minimized, and your expertise takes center stage? Join us on this odyssey, where your curiosity becomes your greatest asset, and the ordinary transforms into the extraordinary.

Open the door to "Automate to Elevate" and step into a future where your skills as an accountant are not just recognized but celebrated. The journey begins now—your seat at the forefront of accounting innovation awaits.

Chapter 1: The art of scripting: VBA fundamentals

The basics of VBA scripting in the context of accounting

Visual Basic for Applications (VBA) scripting in the context of accounting is a powerful tool that allows accountants to automate tasks, streamline processes, and enhance efficiency within Excel. Here are the basics:

1. Accessing the VBA editor

- Enable Developer Tab: Click **File**,

File

Choose **More...**

More...

Go to Excel **Options**

Options

Click **Customize Ribbon**

Customise Ribbon

Check "Developer"

Developer

to enable the **Developer** tab.

Developer

- Open VBA Editor: From the Developer tab, click on "Visual Basic" to open the VBA editor.

2. Understanding the VBA environment

- **Project Explorer**: Lists all open workbooks and their components.

- **Code Window**: Where you write, edit, and view your VBA code.

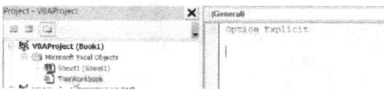

3. Variables and data types

- **Variables**: Used to store and manipulate data. Declare variables using keywords like `Dim`.Here's a very simple example:

```
Sub DeclareVariablesExample()
    ' Declare variables
    Dim myNumber As Integer
    Dim myText As String
    Dim myValue As Double

    ' Assign values to variables
    myNumber = 42
    myText = "Hello, VBA!"
    myValue = 3.14

    ' Display values in the Immediate window (you can view it with
Ctrl + G)
    Debug.Print "Number: " & myNumber
    Debug.Print "Text: " & myText
    Debug.Print "Value: " & myValue
```

End Sub

In this example:

- `myNumber` is declared as an integer.

- `myText` is declared as a string.

- `myValue` is declared as a double (a floating-point number).

You can assign values to these variables and then use them in your VBA code. The `Debug.Print` statements are used to output the values to the Immediate window for demonstration purposes. To view the Immediate window in the VBA editor, you can press `Ctrl + G`.

Remember that VBA is not case-sensitive, so `myNumber` and `MyNumber` would be considered the same variable. It's a good practice to use meaningful names for your variables to make your code more readable.

- Data Types: Specify the type of data a variable can hold (e.g., Integer, String, Double). In VBA, you can use the `As` keyword to specify the type of data a variable can hold. Here's a simple example:

```
Sub SpecifyDataTypeExample()
    ' Declare variables with specified data types
    Dim myInteger As Integer
    Dim myDouble As Double
    Dim myString As String
    Dim myBoolean As Boolean

    ' Assign values to variables
    myInteger = 42
    myDouble = 3.14
    myString = "Hello, VBA!"
    myBoolean = True

    ' Display values in the Immediate window
    Debug.Print "Integer: " & myInteger
    Debug.Print "Double: " & myDouble
    Debug.Print "String: " & myString
    Debug.Print "Boolean: " & myBoolean
```

End Sub

In this example:

- `myInteger` is declared as an integer using `As Integer`.

- `myDouble` is declared as a double using `As Double`.

- `myString` is declared as a string using `As String`.

- `myBoolean` is declared as a boolean using `As Boolean`.

By specifying the data type, you inform VBA about the kind of values the variable will hold, which can help catch potential errors and make your code more robust. Always choose the appropriate data type based on the kind of data you expect the variable to store.

4. Excel object model

- Objects: Everything in Excel is an object (Workbook, Worksheet, Range). In VBA (Visual Basic for Applications), an object is a variable that represents a specific type of entity in the Excel application, such as a worksheet, a range, or a chart. Here's a simple example using the `Range` object:

```
Sub ObjectExample()
    ' Declare a Worksheet object
    Dim myWorksheet As Worksheet

    ' Set the Worksheet object to refer to the first sheet in the
workbook
    Set myWorksheet = ThisWorkbook.Sheets(1)

    ' Declare a Range object within the Worksheet
    Dim myRange As Range

    ' Set the Range object to refer to cells A1:B3 in the
specified worksheet
    Set myRange = myWorksheet.Range("A1:B3")

    ' Perform an action with the Range object
    myRange.Value = "Hello, VBA!"
```

```
    ' Display a message
    MsgBox 'Values have been set in cells A1:B3 of the first
sheet."
End Sub
```

In this example:

- `myWorksheet` is declared as a **Worksheet** object.

- `myRange` is declared as a **Range** object.

The `Set` keyword is used to assign objects. The `ThisWorkbook.Sheets(1)` part refers to the first sheet in the workbook. The `Range("A1:B3")` part refers to a specific range within that worksheet.

The code sets the value of the specified range to "**Hello, VBA!**" and displays a message box.

This is a basic example, and in a real-world scenario, you would often work with various objects like `Workbook`, `Worksheet`, `Range`, `Chart`, etc., to manipulate Excel data and objects.

- Properties and Methods: Objects have properties (attributes) and methods (actions) that you can manipulate using VBA. Properties and methods are features of objects in VBA. Properties represent characteristics or attributes of an object, while methods are actions or operations that can be performed on an object. Let's consider a simple example using the `Range` object:

```
Sub PropertiesAndMethodsExample()
    ' Declare a Worksheet object
    Dim myWorksheet As Worksheet

    ' Set the Worksheet object to refer to the active sheet
    Set myWorksheet = ActiveSheet

    ' Declare a Range object within the Worksheet
    Dim myRange As Range

    ' Set the Range object to refer to cell A1
    Set myRange = myWorksheet.Range("A1")
```

```vba
' Example of using properties
Debug.Print "Address of the Range: " & myRange.Address
Debug.Print "Value in the Range: " & myRange.Value

' Example of using methods
myRange.ClearContents
MsgBox "Content of cell A1 has been cleared."

End Sub
```

In this example:

- `myWorksheet` is declared as a `Worksheet` object.

- `myRange` is declared as a `Range` object.

We use the `Set` keyword to assign objects.

Here's how we use properties and methods:

- Properties:

  - `myRange.Address`: Returns the address of the range.

  - `myRange.Value`: Returns the value in the range.

- Methods:

  - `myRange.ClearContents`: Clears the contents of the range.

The `Debug.Print` statement prints information to the Immediate window, and the `MsgBox` displays a message box.

This is a basic example, and in practical scenarios, you'd often use more properties and methods to manipulate data and objects in Excel.

5. Working with Cells and Ranges

- Selecting Cells: Use `Range` to reference cells (e.g., `Range("A1")`). In VBA, you can use the `Select` method to select cells or ranges. Here's a simple example that demonstrates how to select cells:

```
Sub SelectCellsExample()
    ' Select a single cell
    Range("A1").Select

    ' Select a range of cells
    Range("B2:D4").Select

    ' Select multiple non-contiguous cells
    Range("E5, F6, G7").Select

    ' Select an entire row
    Rows(8).Select

    ' Select an entire column
    Columns("H").Select

    ' Clear the selection
    Selection.Clear

    ' Display a message
    MsgBox "Cell selection has been demonstrated."
End Sub
```

In this example:

- `Range("A1").Select`: Selects the cell in column A, row 1.

- `Range("B2:D4").Select`: Selects the range of cells from B2 to D4.

- `Range("E5, F6, G7").Select`: Selects multiple non-contiguous cells.

- `Rows(8).Select`: Selects the entire row in row 8.

- `Columns("H").Select`: Selects the entire column in column H.

Finally, `Selection.Clear` is used to clear the current selection, and a message box is displayed.

Please note that using `Select` is often not necessary, and it's generally more efficient to work directly with the ranges without selecting them. However, for demonstration purposes, the `Select` method is shown here.

- Manipulating Data: Change cell values, formats, or formulas using VBA. In VBA, you can change cell values, formats, or formulas using various properties and methods. Here's a simple example that demonstrates how to perform these actions:

```
Sub ChangeCellDataExample()
    ' Change cell values
    Range("A1").Value = "New Value"
    Range("B2:D4").Value = 123

    ' Change cell formats
    Range("E5").NumberFormat = "0.00"
    Range("F6").Font.Bold = True
    Range("G7").Interior.Color = RGB(255, 0, 0)

    ' Change cell formulas
    Range("H8").Formula = "=SUM(B2:D4)"
    Range("I9").FormulaR1C1 = "=A1 + B1"

    ' Display a message
    MsgBox "Cell values, formats, and formulas have been changed."
End Sub
```

In this example:

- `Range("A1").Value = "New Value"` sets the value of cell A1 to "New Value".

- `Range("B2:D4").Value = 123` sets the values of the range B2:D4 to 123.

- `Range("E5").NumberFormat = "0.00"` changes the number format of cell E5 to display two decimal places.

- `Range("F6").Font.Bold = True` makes the font bold in cell F6.

- `Range("G7").Interior.Color = RGB(255, 0, 0)` changes the background color of cell G7 to red.

- `Range("H8").Formula = "=SUM(B2:D4)"` sets a formula in cell H8 to sum the values in the range B2:D4.

- `Range("I9").FormulaR1C1 = "=A1 + B1"` sets a formula in cell I9 to sum the values in cells A1 and B1.

The `MsgBox` displays a message box to indicate that the changes have been made.

Keep in mind that these are basic examples, and in real-world scenarios, you might use more complex logic and references based on your specific needs.

6. Control structures

- If...Then...Else Statements: Make decisions based on conditions. The `If...Then...Else` statement in VBA allows you to conditionally execute code based on a specified condition. Here's a simple example:

```
Sub IfThenElseExample()
    ' Declare a variable
    Dim myNumber As Integer

    ' Assign a value to the variable
    myNumber = 42

    ' Check the condition using If...Then...Else
    If myNumber > 50 Then
        ' Code to execute if the condition is true
        MsgBox "The number is greater than 50."
    Else
        ' Code to execute if the condition is false
        MsgBox "The number is 50 or less."
    End If
End Sub
```

In this example:

- `myNumber` is declared as an integer variable.

- It is assigned a value of 42.

- The `If...Then...Else` statement checks whether `myNumber` is greater than 50.

- If the condition is true, a message box is displayed saying "The number is greater than 50."

- If the condition is false, a different message box is displayed saying "The number is 50 or less."

You can adjust the condition and the code within each block to suit your specific requirements. This is a fundamental structure for making decisions in VBA based on conditions.

- For...Next Loops: Perform repetitive actions a specific number of times. The `For...Next` loop in VBA is used to repeat a block of code a specific number of times. Here's a simple example:

```
Sub ForNextLoopExample()
    ' Declare a variable
    Dim i As Integer

    ' Use a For...Next loop to iterate from 1 to 5
    For i = 1 To 5
        ' Code to execute inside the loop
        MsgBox "This is iteration number " & i
    Next i
End Sub
```

In this example:

- The variable `i` is declared as an integer.

- The `For...Next` loop is used to iterate from 1 to 5 (`For i = 1 To 5`).

- Inside the loop, a message box is displayed indicating the current iteration.

The loop will run five times, and each time it runs, the message box will display the current iteration number.

You can customize the loop by changing the starting and ending values (`For i = 1 To 5`), and you can use the loop variable (`i` in this case) within the loop to perform actions that depend on the current iteration.

- Do...Loop Statements: Create loops based on certain conditions. The `Do...Loop` statement in VBA is used for creating loops where the code within the loop continues to execute as long as a specified condition is true. Here's a simple example using a `Do While` loop:

```vba
Sub DoLoopExample()
    ' Declare a variable
    Dim counter As Integer

    ' Initialize the counter
    counter = 1

    ' Use a Do While loop to iterate until the counter is less
than or equal to 5
    Do While counter <= 5
        ' Code to execute inside the loop
        MsgBox "This is iteration number " & counter

        ' Increment the counter
        counter = counter + 1
    Loop
End Sub
```

In this example:

- The variable `counter` is declared as an integer.

- The `Do While` loop is used to iterate as long as the condition `counter <= 5` is true.

- Inside the loop, a message box is displayed indicating the current iteration.

- The `counter` is incremented within the loop to ensure that the loop eventually exits.

The loop will run five times, and each time it runs, the message box will display the current iteration number.

You can customize the loop by changing the condition inside the `Do While` statement based on your specific requirements.

7. Procedures and functions

- Subroutines (Subs): Contain a series of instructions. Used for tasks without returning a value. A subroutine, often referred to as a "Sub" in VBA, is a block of code that performs a specific task. Here's a simple example of a subroutine:

```
Sub MySimpleSubroutine()
    ' Code to be executed
    MsgBox "Hello, I am a simple subroutine!"
End Sub
```

In this example:

- `Sub MySimpleSubroutine()` declares the beginning of the subroutine named "MySimpleSubroutine."

- `MsgBox "Hello, I am a simple subroutine!"` is the code that the subroutine executes. In this case, it displays a message box saying "Hello, I am a simple subroutine!"

You can then call this subroutine from another procedure or execute it directly. For example:

```
Sub CallMySubroutine()
    ' Call the MySimpleSubroutine
    MySimpleSubroutine
End Sub
```

In the second code snippet:

- `Sub CallMySubroutine()` declares another subroutine.

- `MySimpleSubroutine` is the line that calls the previously defined `MySimpleSubroutine` subroutine.

When you run the `CallMySubroutine` subroutine, it will execute the code within `MySimpleSubroutine` and display the message box.

Subroutines are used to organize code into manageable blocks, making your VBA projects more modular and easier to maintain.

- Functions: Return a value and are useful for calculations. In VBA, a function is a block of code that performs a specific task and returns a value. Here's a simple example of a function:

```
Function AddNumbers(x As Integer, y As Integer) As Integer
    ' Code to be executed
    AddNumbers = x + y
End Function
```

In this example:

- `Function AddNumbers(x As Integer, y As Integer) As Integer` declares the beginning of the function named "AddNumbers." It takes two parameters, `x` and `y`, both of type Integer, and returns an Integer.

- `AddNumbers = x + y` is the code that the function executes. It adds the values of `x` and `y` and assigns the result to the function's name (`AddNumbers`). This line effectively sets the return value of the function.

You can then use this function in your code. For example:

```
Sub CallMyFunction()
    ' Declare variables
    Dim result As Integer

    ' Call the AddNumbers function
    result = AddNumbers(5, 3)

    ' Display the result
    MsgBox "The result is: " & result
End Sub
```

In this second code snippet:

- `Sub CallMyFunction()` declares a subroutine.

- `result = AddNumbers(5, 3)` calls the `AddNumbers` function with the arguments 5 and 3. The result is stored in the variable `result`.

- `MsgBox "The result is: " & result` displays a message box with the result.

When you run the `CallMyFunction` subroutine, it will use the `AddNumbers` function to add 5 and 3, and the result (8) will be displayed in the message box. Functions are useful for performing calculations or tasks that return a result.

8. Debugging

- Breakpoints: Pause code execution at a specific line. Debugging using breakpoints in VBA allows you to pause the execution of your code at a specific line, giving you the opportunity to inspect variables, check the flow of your program, and identify issues. Here's a simple example:

```
Sub DebuggingExample()
    ' Declare variables
    Dim x As Integer
    Dim y As Integer
    Dim result As Integer

    ' Assign values to variables
    x = 5
    y = 3

    ' Set a breakpoint on the next line
    Stop

    ' Call the AddNumbers function
    result = AddNumbers(x, y)

    ' Display the result
    MsgBox "The result is: " & result
End Sub

Function AddNumbers(x As Integer, y As Integer) As Integer
    ' Code to be executed
    AddNumbers = x + y
End Function
```

In this example:

- `Sub DebuggingExample()` is a subroutine that calls the `AddNumbers` function.

- `Stop` is used to set a breakpoint. When the code reaches this line during execution, it will pause, allowing you to inspect variables and step through the code.

- `result = AddNumbers(x, y)` calls the `AddNumbers` function with the arguments `x` and `y`.

- `MsgBox "The result is: " & result` displays a message box with the result.

Here's how you can use breakpoints:

1. Run the `DebuggingExample` subroutine.
2. When the code reaches the `Stop` line, the execution will pause.
3. Use the VBA editor to inspect the values of variables, step through the code, and identify any issues.
4. Continue execution or stop debugging as needed.

To run the code with breakpoints, you can use the "Run" button in the VBA editor toolbar or press `F5`. To step through the code line by line, you can use the "Step Into" button or press `F8`.

- Immediate Window: Test code and variables interactively. The Immediate Window in VBA is a powerful tool that allows you to interact with the VBA environment in real-time. It provides an interactive command-line interface where you can execute statements, evaluate expressions, and inspect the values of variables during runtime. The Immediate Window is particularly useful for debugging, testing, and experimenting with code without the need to modify your actual VBA modules.

Here are some key features and use cases of the Immediate Window:

- You can execute individual VBA statements directly in the Immediate Window, allowing you to test code snippets or run specific commands without the need to create a separate procedure.

```
Debug.Print "Hello, Immediate Window!"
```

- You can evaluate expressions to check the result or value of a particular calculation or operation.

```
? 5 + 3
```

- You can inspect the current values of variables by simply typing the variable name and pressing Enter.

```
? x
```

- During the execution of a subroutine or function, you can pause the code using the `Stop` statement or by setting breakpoints. Once paused, you can use the Immediate Window to check variable values, execute commands, and understand the state of your program.

- You can use `Debug.Print` statements in your code to output messages, variable values, or other information to the Immediate Window. This is an effective way to log information for debugging purposes.

```
Debug.Print "The value of x is: " & x
```

- The Immediate Window is a quick way to test and experiment with code without modifying your actual VBA modules. This is especially useful for trying out different approaches or troubleshooting issues interactively.

To open the Immediate Window in the VBA editor, you can press `Ctrl + G` or select "Immediate Window" from the "View" menu. The Immediate Window enhances the flexibility and interactivity of the VBA development environment, making it a valuable tool for developers working with Excel and other Office applications.

9. Event handling

- Worksheet Events: Trigger actions based on changes in the worksheet (e.g., cell value change). In VBA, you can use event handling to trigger actions based on changes in the worksheet. One common event is the `Worksheet_Change` event, which is triggered whenever a cell in the worksheet is modified. Here's a simple example:

```
Private Sub Worksheet_Change(ByVal Target As Range)
    ' This subroutine is automatically triggered when a cell is
changed

    ' Check if the changed cell is in column A
    If Not Intersect(Target, Columns("A")) Is Nothing Then
        ' Perform an action when a cell in column A is changed
        MsgBox "A cell in column A has been changed."
    End If
End Sub
```

Here's how to set up this example:

1. Open the Excel workbook where you want to implement the event handling.

2. Press `Alt + F11` to open the VBA editor.

3. In the Project Explorer, find the worksheet where you want to handle changes.

4. Right-click on the sheet, and choose "View Code."

5. Paste the provided code into the code window for the selected sheet.

Now, whenever a cell in column A of that sheet is changed, a message box will appear.

You can customize the code to perform different actions based on the conditions you need. For example, you might want to perform specific calculations, update other cells, or trigger more complex procedures.

It's important to note that the code should be placed in the code module for the specifc sheet where you want the event to be handled (`Worksheet_Change`). This ensures that the event is specific to that sheet.

- Workbook Events: Respond to events like opening or closing the workbook. In VBA, you can use workbook events to respond to actions such as opening or closing the workbook. Here's a simple example using the `Workbook_Open` and `Workbook_BeforeClose` events:

```
Private Sub Workbook_Open()
    ' This subroutine is automatically triggered when the workbook
is opened
    MsgBox "Welcome! The workbook has been opened."
End Sub

Private Sub Workbook_BeforeClose(Cancel As Boolean)
    ' This subroutine is automatically triggered before the
workbook is closed
    MsgBox "Goodbye! The workbook is about to be closed."
End Sub
```

Here's how to set up this example:

1. Open the Excel workbook where you want to implement the workbook events.

2. Press `Alt + F11` to open the VBA editor.

3. In the Project Explorer, find the "ThisWorkbook" object under the workbook you are working with.

4. Double-click on "ThisWorkbook" to open its code window.

5. Paste the provided code into the code window.

Now, when you open the workbook, a message box will appear, and when you try to close the workbook, another message box will appear.

You can customize the code within these event procedures to perform specific actions when the workbook is opened or closed. For example, you might want to set up initial conditions, load data, or save changes before closing.

Remember that these events are specific to the workbook, and the code should be placed in the code module for the "ThisWorkbook" object.

10. Integration with Excel formulas

- Worksheet Functions: Let's start with a simple example in which we use VBA to incorporate and manipulate an Excel function. In this case, we'll use the `SUM` function to add values from a range of cells.

1. Open Excel and press `Alt + F11` to open the Visual Basic for Applications (VBA) editor.

2. In the VBA editor, insert a new module by right-clicking on any item in the Project Explorer, selecting "Insert," and then choosing "Module."

3. In the module, enter the following code:

```
Sub SumExample()
    ' Declare variables
    Dim sumResult As Double
    Dim rng As Range

    ' Set the range to sum (adjust the range as needed)
    Set rng = Range("A1:A5")

    ' Use the SUM function in VBA to calculate the sum
    sumResult = Application.WorksheetFunction.Sum(rng)

    ' Display the result in a message box
    MsgBox "Sum of the range: " & sumResult
End Sub
```

4. Close the VBA editor and return to Excel.

5. Press `Alt + F8` to open the "Macro" dialog box, select "SumExample," and click "Run."

This example demonstrates how to use the `SUM` function in VBA to calculate the sum of values in a specified range (`A1:A5` in this case). The result is then displayed in a message box.

You can customize the code by adjusting the range (`Set rng = Range("your_range_here")`) or using different Excel functions depending on your requirements. This is just a basic example to get you started with incorporating Excel functions in VBA.

- Custom Functions: Creating custom functions in VBA allows you to streamline complex calculations by encapsulating them into a single function. Here's a simple example of a custom function that calculates the factorial of a given number:

1. Open Excel and press `Alt + F11` to open the Visual Basic for Applications (VBA) editor.

2. In the VBA editor, insert a new module by right-clicking on any item in the Project Explorer, selecting "Insert," and then choosing "Module."

3. In the module, enter the following code:

```
Function CalculateFactorial(ByVal n As Integer) As Double
    ' Calculate the factorial of a number
    If n = 0 Then
        CalculateFactorial = 1
    Else
        CalculateFactorial = n * CalculateFactorial(n - 1)
    End If
End Function
```

4. Close the VBA editor and return to Excel.

5. Now, you can use this custom function in your worksheet. For example, in cell A1, enter a number (e.g., 5), and in cell B1, enter the following formula:

```
=CalculateFactorial(A1)
```

6. Press Enter, and you should see the factorial of the number in cell B1.

This example demonstrates a simple custom function called `CalculateFactorial`. It takes an integer (`n`) as input and recursively calculates the factorial of that number. You can create your own custom functions in a similar manner to streamline complex calculations in Excel. Customize the function based on your specific requirements.

11. Error handling

- On Error Statements: In VBA, the `On Error` statement is used to handle errors gracefully and prevent script crashes. Here's a simple example of how you can use `On Error` to manage errors:

```
Sub ErrorHandlingExample()
    On Error GoTo ErrorHandler

    ' Your main code here

    ' Simulate a division by zero error
    Dim result As Double
    result = 10 / 0

    ' Continue with the rest of your code if there is no error
    MsgBox "Result: " & result

    ' Jump to the ExitSub label to skip the error handler in case
of no error
    GoTo ExitSub

ErrorHandler:
    ' Hancle the error gracefully
    MsgBox "An error occurred: " & Err.Description, vbExclamation

ExitSub:
    ' Clean up or perform any necessary actions before exiting the
sub

End Sub
```

In this example:
- The `On Error GoTo ErrorHandler` statement is used to direct the script to the `ErrorHandler` label if an error occurs.

- The main code executes, and if there's an error (in this case, a division by zero error is simulated), the script jumps to the `ErrorHandler` label.

- In the `ErrorHandler` section, you can include code to handle the error gracefully. In this case, a message box is displayed with information about the error.

- The `ExitSub` label is used to indicate where the script should go after handling the error. This label is used to skip the error handler if there was no error.

This is a basic example, and in a real-world scenario, you might want to include more detailed error handling and possibly log errors for later analysis. The key is to use `On Error` to anticipate potential issues and handle them in a way that prevents the script from crashing.

- Debugging Tools: Identify and fix errors using debugging tools. Debugging is an essential part of programming, and VBA provides several tools to help identify and fix errors. Here's a simple example that demonstrates the use of debugging tools:

```
Sub DebuggingExample()
    Dim x As Integer
    Dim y As Integer
    Dim result As Integer

    ' Initialize variables
    x = 10
    y = 0

    ' Attempt to perform division
    result = x / y

    ' Display the result
    MsgBox "Result: " & result
End Sub
```

In this example, there's a deliberate error: attempting to divide by zero (`y = 0`). To identify and fix the error, you can use the following debugging tools:

1. Set a Breakpoint:

- Place the cursor on the line `result = x / y`.

- Press `F9` or click in the left margin next to the line number. This sets a breakpoint, and the code will pause execution just before this line.

2. Run the Code:

- Press `F5` to run the code.

3. Debugging Toolbar:

- When the code encounters the division by zero, it pauses, and the VBA editor is brought to the front.

- Use the debugging toolbar (or menu) to navigate through the code.

- Press `F8` to execute the code line-by-line.

- Hover over variables to see their current values.

4. Immediate Window:

- Press `Ctrl + G` to open the Immediate Window.

- In the Immediate Window, you can type and execute immediate statements.

- For example, you can type `? x` and press `Enter` to see the current value of the variable `x`.

5. Locals Window:

- Press `Ctrl + L` to open the Locals Window.

- The Locals Window shows the values of all variables in the current scope.

6. Fix the Error:

- Change `y = 0` to a non-zero value (e.g., `y = 2`).

7. Continue Execution:

- Press `F5` to continue running the code until completion.

Using breakpoints, stepping through code, and inspecting variable values can help you identify and fix errors in your VBA scripts. These are just a few basic debugging tools, and the VBA editor offers additional features for more advanced debugging.

12. Security considerations

- Macro Security: Be aware of security settings and ensure macros are enabled. Macro security settings in Microsoft Excel, as well as other Office applications, are typically managed through the Trust Center. Here's how you can access and configure macro security settings:

1. Open Excel: Launch Microsoft Excel on your computer.

2. Access the Trust Center:

   - Click on the "File" tab in the Excel ribbon.

   - Select "Options" at the bottom of the left-hand menu. This opens the Excel Options dialog.

3. Navigate to the Trust Center:

   - In the Excel Options dialog, click on "Trust Center" in the left-hand menu.

4. Access Macro Settings:

   - Within the Trust Center, click on the "Trust Center Settings" button.

5. Configure Macro Security:

   - In the Trust Center, select "Macro Settings" in the left-hand menu.

   - Here, you'll find various options for configuring macro security levels:

     - **Disable all macros without notification (High)**: No macros are allowed to run.

     - **Disable all macros with notification (Medium)**: Users are prompted to enable or disable macros.

     - **Enable all macros (not recommended, potentially dangerous code can run)**: Macros run without any prompts.

     - **Enable all macros except digitally signed macros**: Macros are allowed to run, but only if they are digitally signed by a trusted source.

     - **Trust access to the VBA project object model**: Allows programmatic access to the VBA object model.

6. Apply Changes:

   - After selecting your desired security level, click **"OK"** to apply the changes.

7. Optional: Configure Trusted Locations:

   - In the Trust Center, you can also configure "Trusted Locations" to specify folders on your computer or network where macros are considered safe.

By carefully configuring these settings, you can manage the security of macros in Excel. It's generally recommended to keep macro security at a level that balances security and functionality. For most users, the "Disable all macros with notification" (Medium) setting is a good compromise, as it prompts users to enable macros on a case-by-case basis.

Always exercise caution when enabling macros, especially in documents received from unknown or untrusted sources. Be sure to review the security settings periodically and keep your software, including Microsoft Office, up to date to benefit from the latest security enhancements.

   - Code Protection: Protect your VBA code to prevent unauthorized access. Protecting your VBA code involves taking measures to prevent unauthorized access, viewing, and modification of your code. Here are a few techniques you can use to enhance the security of your VBA code:

1. Password Protect the VBA Project:

   - Open the Excel workbook containing your VBA code.

   - Press `Alt + F11` to open the VBA editor.

   - In the VBA editor, go to the "Tools" menu and select "VBAProject Properties."

   - In the "Protection" tab, check the "Lock project for viewing" box.

   - Enter and confirm a password.

   - Click "OK" to apply the protection.

This will prompt users for a password when attempting to view or modify the VBA code.

2. Compile VBA Code to Binary Format (P-Code):

- In the VBA editor, go to the "Debug" menu and select "Compile VBAProject."

- This step converts your VBA code to a binary format (P-Code), making it more challenging to reverse engineer.

3. Use VBA Code Obfuscation:

- Rename variables, functions, and subroutines to make the code less readable.

- Avoid using meaningful names that could reveal the purpose of the code.

- Break down complex operations into simpler, less obvious steps.

4. Remove Unused Code:

- Remove any unused or unnecessary code to reduce the overall footprint of your VBA project.

- This makes it more difficult for someone to understand the purpose of the code.

5. Convert Sensitive Information into Constants:

- If your code involves sensitive information (e.g., API keys), consider converting them into constants and storing them in a secure location outside the VBA code.

6. Regularly Backup Your Code:

- Keep backups of your original, unprotected code in a secure location.

- This ensures that even if you forget the password or encounter issues, you have a safe copy.

7. Consider External Protection Tools:

- There are third-party tools available that claim to provide enhanced protection for VBA code. These tools may offer additional features beyond the built-in protection provided by Excel.

It's important to note that while these measures can add an extra layer of security, no protection method is entirely foolproof. Determined attackers may still find ways to access or reverse engineer your code. Therefore, it's essential to strike a balance between protecting your code and ensuring that you can maintain and understand it yourself.

Always keep backups of your unprotected code, and choose protection methods that align with the level of security you require for your particular use case.

13. Real-world application

- Automate Data Entry: Develop scripts for efficient data input. Automating data entry in Excel using VBA can significantly improve efficiency. Below is a simple example that demonstrates how to automate data entry for a list of employees into an Excel worksheet.

1. Create a new Excel workbook:

Open Excel and create a new workbook.

2. Insert a new module:

Press `Alt + F11` to open the VBA editor. Right-click on any item in the Project Explorer, select "Insert," and then choose "Module."

3. Enter the following VBA code:

```vba
Sub AutomateDataEntry()
    ' Define variables for employee data
    Dim employeeName As String
    Dim employeeID As Integer
    Dim employeeSalary As Double

    ' Set up loop for data entry (adjust the loop count as needed)
    For i = 1 To 3 ' Entering data for three employees as an
example
        ' Prompt user for employee data
        employeeName = InputBox("Enter the name of Employee " & i
& ":")
        employeeID = InputBox("Enter the ID of Employee " & i &
":")
        employeeSalary = InputBox("Enter the salary of Employee "
& i & ":")

        ' Enter data into the worksheet
        Cells(i, 1).Value = employeeName
        Cells(i, 2).Value = employeeID
        Cells(i, 3).Value = employeeSalary
    Next i

    MsgBox "Data entry complete!", vbInformation
End Sub
```

4. Run the macro:

Close the VBA editor and return to Excel. Press `Alt + F8`, select "AutomateDataEntry," and click "Run."

5. Follow the prompts:

The script will prompt you to enter the name, ID, and salary for each employee. The entered data will be automatically populated in the first three rows of columns A, B, and C.

This example uses a simple loop to prompt the user for employee data and then enters that data into the worksheet. Adjust the loop count and data entry fields according to your specific requirements.

Remember to save your workbook before running the script, as the InputBox prompts may not allow you to save your work until they are closed.

This is a basic example, and depending on your specific needs, you can expand the script to handle more complex data entry tasks or interact with external data sources.

- Enhance Reporting: Streamline report generation processes. Certainly! Below is a simple example of how you can enhance reporting in Excel by streamlining the process using VBA. This example assumes you want to generate a basic report that calculates the total sales for each product category.

1. Create a new Excel workbook:

   Open Excel and create a new workbook.

2. Insert a new module:

   Press `Alt + F11` to open the VBA editor. Right-click on any item in the Project Explorer, select "Insert," and then choose "Module."

3. Enter the following VBA code:

```
Sub GenerateSalesReport()
  ' Declare variables
  Dim wsData As Worksheet
```

```
Dim wsReport As Worksheet
Dim lastRow As Long
Dim productCategory As String
Dim totalSales As Double

' Set references to worksheets
Set wsData = ThisWorkbook.Sheets("DataSheet") ' Change
"DataSheet" to the name of your data sheet
Set wsReport = ThisWorkbook.Sheets.Add ' Create a new sheet
for the report
wsReport.Name = "SalesReport"

' Set headers for the report
wsReport.Cells(1, 1).Value = "Product Category"
wsReport.Cells(1, 2).Value = "Total Sales"

' Find the last row with data in the data sheet
lastRow = wsData.Cells(wsData.Rows.Count, "A").End(xlUp).Row

' Loop through the data and calculate total sales for each
product category
For i = 2 To lastRow ' Assuming data starts from row 2
    productCategory = wsData.Cells(i, 1).Value ' Assuming
product category is in column A
    totalSales = totalSales + wsData.Cells(i, 2).Value '
Assuming sales amount is in column B
Next i

' Populate the report with the calculated data
wsReport.Cells(2, 1).Value = productCategory
wsReport.Cells(2, 2).Value = totalSales

' Format the report for better readability (optional)
wsReport.Columns("A:B").AutoFit

MsgBox "Sales report generated successfully!", vbInformation
```

End Sub

4. Run the macro:

Close the VBA editor and return to Excel. Press `Alt + F8`, select "GenerateSalesReport," and click "Run."

5. Review the generated report:

The script will create a new sheet named "SalesReport" with the product category and total sales information.

This is a basic example, and you can customize the code according to your specific reporting needs. For a more robust solution, you might want to consider incorporating dynamic range names, handling different data structures, and providing user-friendly interfaces for report generation.

- Ensure Accuracy: Implement error-checking routines for precise results. Ensuring accuracy in VBA involves implementing error-checking routines to catch and handle potential issues in your code. Below is a simple example that demonstrates how to add error-checking routines for precise results. In this example, I'll create a VBA script that divides two numbers and handles potential errors, such as div ision by zero.

1. Open Excel and create a new workbook:

Open Excel and create a new workbook.

2. Insert a new module:

Press `Alt + F11` to open the VBA editor. Right-click on any item in the Project Explorer, select "Insert," and then choose "Module."

3. Enter the following VBA code:

```vba
Function DivideNumbers(ByVal numerator As Double, ByVal
denominator As Double) As Variant
    ' Function to divide two numbers and handle errors
    On Error Resume Next ' Enable error handling

    ' Initialize result
    Dim result As Variant

    ' Check for division by zero
    If denominator = 0 Then
        result = CVErr(xlDiv0) ' Return a #DIV/0! error value
    Else
        result = numerator / denominator ' Perform the division
    End If

    On Error GoTo 0 ' Disable error handling

    ' Return the result
    DivideNumbers = result
End Function
```

4. Use the function in a worksheet:

   In your Excel worksheet, enter numbers in cells A1 and B1, and use the following formula in another cell (e.g., C1):

```
=DivideNumbers(A1, B1)
```

5. Review the result:

   The `DivideNumbers` function returns the result of the division or a `#DIV/0!` error if the denominator is zero.

In this example:

- The `On Error Resume Next` statement is used to enable error handling.

- The division is performed inside a conditional statement that checks for division by zero.

- If a division by zero is detected, the function returns a `#DIV/0!` error using `CVErr(xlDiv0)`.

- The `On Error GoTo 0` statement is used to disable error handling after the error check.

This simple error-checking routine ensures that the division operation is performed with accurate and expected results. Depending on your specific requirements, you can extend error checking to handle various types of errors that might occur in your code. Always tailor error-handling routines to the specific needs and potential issues of your VBA scripts.

Mastering these basics empowers accountants to leverage VBA scripting for increased efficiency, accuracy, and customized automation in their accounting tasks within Excel.

Dive into the anatomy of a VBA script

Certainly! Let's dive into the anatomy of a VBA script to understand its structure and components. A VBA script, also known as a macro, is a set of instructions written in the Visual Basic for Applications language. Here's a breakdown of its key elements:

1. Subroutine Declaration:

- The script begins with a `Sub` (Subroutine) declaration, indicating the start of the main block of code.

- Example:

```
Sub MyMacro()
```

2. Variable Declarations:

- Variables store and manipulate data. They need to be declared using the `Dim` keyword.

- Example:

```
Dim myVariable As Integer
```

3. Object Variables:

- In Excel VBA, you often work with objects (worksheets, ranges, etc.). Declare object variables using the `Dim` keyword.

- Example:

```
Dim ws As Worksheet
```

4. Procedure Body:

- The main block of code where instructions are written. It is enclosed between the `Sub` and `End Sub` statements.

- Example:

```
Sub MyMacro()
    ' Code goes here
End Sub
```

5. Comments:

- Comments provide information about the code and are not executed. They are preceded by an apostrophe (`'`) or use the `Rem` keyword.

- Example:

```
' This is a comment
Rem Another way to comment
```

6. Object Manipulation:

- Use VBA to manipulate Excel objects like worksheets, ranges, cells, etc.

- Example:

```
Set ws = Worksheets("Sheet1")
ws.Range("A1").Value = "Hello, World!"
```

7. Control Flow Statements:

 - Control the flow of execution using statements like `**If...Then...Else**`, `**For...Next**`, and `**Do...Loop**`.

 - Example:

```
If myVariable > 10 Then
    ' Code block when the condition is true
Else
    ' Code block when the condition is false
End If
```

8. Functions:

 - Functions return a value and are declared using the `**Function**` keyword. They are often used for calculations.

 - Example:

```
Function AddNumbers(x As Integer, y As Integer) As Integer
    AddNumbers = x + y
End Function
```

9. Loops:

 - Use loops like `**For...Next**` or `**Do...Loop**` to repeat a set of instructions.

 - Example:

```
For i = 1 To 10
    ' Code block to repeat
Next i
```

10. Error Handling:

 - Implement error handling using statements like `**On Error Resume Next**` to gracefully manage errors.

 - Example:

```
On Error Resume Next
' Code that might cause an error
On Error GoTo 0 ' Resets error handling to default
```

11. Procedure Call:

- If you have defined functions or other subroutines, you can call them within your script.

- Example:

```
result = AddNumbers(5, 3)
```

12. End Statement:

- The `End Sub` statement marks the end of the subroutine.

- Example:

```
End Sub
```

By understanding these components, you can begin creating powerful VBA scripts tailored to automate and enhance various accounting tasks in Excel. Each element plays a crucial role in structuring the script and achieving the desired outcomes.

Introduce the Excel object model and its relevance to accounting tasks

The Excel Object Model is a hierarchical structure that represents the elements of Microsoft Excel, allowing users to interact with and manipulate the various components of an Excel application. Understanding the Excel Object Model is essential for anyone looking to leverage Visual Basic for Applications (VBA) scripting in accounting tasks.

Excel Object Model Hierarchy:

1. Application:

- The top-level object in the hierarchy, representing the entire Excel application.

- Example:

```
Dim excelApp As Excel.Application
Set excelApp = New Excel.Application
```

2. Workbook:

- Represents an Excel workbook, which can contain multiple sheets.

- Example:

```
Dim workbook As Excel.Workbook
Set workbook =
excelApp.Workbooks.Open("C:\Path\To\Workbook.xlsx")
```

3. Worksheet:

- Represents an individual sheet within a workbook.

- Example:

```
Dim worksheet As Excel.Worksheet
Set worksheet = workbook.Worksheets("Sheet1")
```

4. Range:

- Represents a group of cells on a worksheet.

- Example:

```
Dim dataRange As Excel.Range
Set dataRange = worksheet.Range("A1:B10")
```

5. Cell:

- Represents an individual cell within a range.

- Example:

```
Dim cell As Excel.Range
Set cell = worksheet.Range("A1")
```

Relevance to Accounting Tasks:

1. Data Entry:

   - Use the Range object to input data into specific cells or ranges programmatically, streamlining data entry processes.

2. Calculations:

   - Leverage the Range object to perform calculations on sets of data, automating complex financial computations.

3. Report Generation:

   - Manipulate worksheets and ranges to dynamically generate reports based on accounting data, ensuring consistency and accuracy.

4. Formatting:

   - Customize the format of cells, ranges, and entire worksheets to enhance the presentation of financial information.

5. Data Validation:

   - Implement data validation through the Range object to ensure that entered data adheres to specific criteria, reducing errors in accounting datasets.

6. Chart Creation:

   - Utilize the Chart object within the Excel Object Model to automate the creation of visual representations of financial data.

7. Data Analysis:

  - Access and manipulate data within ranges to perform advanced data analysis, enabling accountants to derive meaningful insights.

8. Dynamic Dashboards:

  - Combine the power of worksheets, ranges, and charts to create dynamic dashboards that update in real-time based on accounting data changes.

By navigating and manipulating the Excel Object Model through VBA scripting, accountants can automate repetitive tasks, reduce manual errors, and customize Excel to suit their specific accounting needs. This level of automation enhances efficiency, accuracy, and the overall productivity of accounting processes.

A hands-on guide to writing your first simple script

Let's walk through a hands-on guide to writing your first simple VBA script. In this example, we'll create a basic script to automate a common accounting task: summing up a column of numbers.

Step 1: Open the VBA Editor

1. Open Excel and navigate to the Developer tab.

2. If the Developer tab is not visible, enable it in Excel **Options** > **Customize Ribbon**.

3. In the Developer tab, click on "Visual Basic" to open the VBA editor.

Step 2: Create a New Module

1. In the VBA editor, right-click on any item in the Project Explorer (usually on the left).

2. Choose "Insert" and then "Module" to create a new module.

Step 3: Write Your First Script

Now, let's write a simple script to sum the values in column A and display the result in a message box.

```
Sub SumColumnA()
    ' Declare variables
    Dim ws As Worksheet
    Dim lastRow As Long
    Dim sumResult As Double

    ' Set the worksheet
    Set ws = ThisWorkbook.Sheets("Sheet1")  ' Change "Sheet1" to
your actual sheet name

    ' Find the last row with data in column A
    lastRow = ws.Cells(ws.Rows.Count, "A").End(xlUp).Row

    ' Sum the values in column A
    sumResult = Application.WorksheetFunction.Sum(ws.Range("A1:A"
& lastRow))

    ' Display the result in a message box
    MsgBox "The sum of values in column A is: " & sumResult
End Sub
```

Step 4: Run Your Script

1. Close the VBA editor.

2. In Excel, go back to the Developer tab.

3. Click on "Macros," select your macro ("SumColumnA"), and click "Run."

Step 5: Observe the Result

You should see a message box displaying the sum of the values in column A.

Step 6: Customize for Your Needs

Feel free to customize the script according to your specific accounting requirements. You can modify the worksheet, column, or even incorporate user input.

Congratulations! You've just created and executed your first simple VBA script for an accounting task. This serves as a foundation for more complex scripts as you delve deeper into the world of VBA automation.

Chapter 2: Data dance: Automating data entry

The challenges of manual data entry in accounting

Manual data entry in accounting comes with several challenges that can impact accuracy, efficiency, and overall reliability of financial information. Some of the key challenges include:

1. Human error:

- Manual data entry is susceptible to human errors such as typos, transposition errors, and data entry mistakes. These errors can lead to inaccuracies in financial records and, subsequently, financial reports.

2. Time-consuming:

- Manual data entry is time-consuming, especially for large volumes of data. Accountants spend a significant amount of time inputting data, which could be better utilized for analysis, decision-making, and more value-added tasks.

3. Repetitiveness and boredom:

- The repetitive nature of manual data entry tasks can lead to boredom and a decline in focus, increasing the likelihood of errors. This monotony can also contribute to employee dissatisfaction.

4. Lack of scalability:

- Manual data entry is not easily scalable. As the volume of data increases, the time and effort required for manual input grow proportionally. This limitation can be challenging for businesses experiencing growth.

5. Limited data analysis:

- Manual data entry often leaves little time for accountants to analyze data comprehensively. Analysis is crucial for identifying trends, making informed decisions, and providing valuable insights to management.

6. Dependency on individuals:

- When data entry is performed manually, it often relies heavily on specific individuals. This dependency becomes a risk in cases of employee turnover, as knowledge and skills associated with data entry may not be easily transferable.

7. Data security concerns:

- Manual data entry may involve handling sensitive financial information. The risk of unauthorized access, data breaches, or accidental data exposure increases when manual processes are in place.

8. Integration challenges:

- Integrating data across various accounting systems or software may be cumbersome when relying on manual data entry. This can result in inconsistenc es between different platforms and hinder data accuracy.

9. Compliance and reporting risks:

- Errors in manual data entry can lead to compliance issues and reporting errors. This is particularly critical in industries where regulatory compliance is stringent, and financial reports must adhere to specific standards.

10. Costs of rectification:

- Detecting and correcting errors in manually entered data can be costly and time-consuming. It may require extensive efforts to identify the source of errors and rectify discrepancies.

To overcome these challenges, many businesses are increasingly adopting automation and technology solutions, such as accounting software, optical character recognition (OCR) tools, and data validation checks, to streamline data entry processes and enhance accuracy in financial reporting. Automation not only reduces the likelihood of errors but also allows accounting professionals to focus on more strategic and analytical aspects of their roles.

How VBA scripts can streamline and automate data input processes

VBA (Visual Basic for Applications) scripts in Excel can significantly streamline and automate data input processes by eliminating manual data entry, reducing errors, and improving overall efficiency. Here are some ways VBA scripts can be used for data input automation:

1. Form creation:

   - Scenario: You need to input data in a structured manner with a user-friendly interface.

   - Solution: Use VBA to create custom forms or user interfaces that guide users through the data input process. Forms can include input fields, dropdowns, and buttons to automate data entry.

2. Data validation:

   - Scenario: Ensuring data accuracy by validating input against predefined criteria.

   - Solution: Implement VBA scripts to perform data validation checks. For example, you can use VBA to enforce specific formats, ranges, or dependencies between data fields.

3. Automated Data Import:

- Scenario: mporting data from external sources into Excel.

- Solution: Write VBA scripts to automate the import process. This could involve fetching data from databases, web services, or text files and populating Excel worksheets automatically.

4. Dynamic Data Ranges:

- Scenario: Handling dynamic data ranges that change frequently.

- Solution: Use VBA to dynamically adjust data ranges based on the changing nature of your data. This ensures that your scripts work seamlessly even as the amount of data fluctuates.

5. Data Transformation:

- Scenario: Transforming raw data into a structured format.

- Solution: Develop VBA scripts to perform data transformations, such as splitting, merging, or cleaning data, to ensure it conforms to the required structure.

6. Automated Calculations:

- Scenario: Automating calculations based on input data.

- Solution: Use VBA to perform calculations automatically. This is particularly useful for scenarios where multiple calculations need to be performed based on the input data.

7. Data Copying and Pasting:

- Scenario: Copying data from one location to another.

- Solution: Automate copying and pasting of data using VBA. This is helpful for tasks like consolidating data from different sheets or workbooks.

8. Batch Data Entry:

  - Scenario: Entering a large amount of similar data.

  - Solution: Develop VBA scripts to automate batch data entry. For example, you could create a script that populates a column with a series of values or duplicates a set of data.

9. Data Cleaning:

  - Scenario: Cleaning and standardizing data.

  - Solution: Use VBA to automate data cleaning processes, such as removing duplicates, handling outliers, or correcting formatting issues.

10. Error Handling:

  - Scenario: Minimizing errors in data input.

  - Solution: Implement robust error-handling routines in your VBA scripts to catch and address potential issues, ensuring the reliability of your automated processes.

11. Integration with Other Applications:

  - Scenario: Exchanging data with other applications.

  - Solution: Use VBA to automate interactions between Excel and other applications, enabling seamless data exchange.

By leveraging the power of VBA, you can create custom solutions that cater to your specific data input requirements, resulting in more efficient and accurate data management processes.

Customizable scripts for common data entry tasks

Creating customizable scripts for common data entry tasks in VBA involves designing flexible and adaptable code that can be easily adjusted to suit various scenarios. Here's a step-by-step guide to building such scripts:

1. Identify Common Data Entry Tasks:

   - List the common data entry tasks that you frequently perform. For example, entering data into specific cells, importing data, performing calculations, or validating inputs.

2. Plan for Flexibility:

   - Think about how to make your scripts adaptable to different situations. Consider using parameters and variables that can be easily changed to customize the behavior of the script.

3. Use Input Parameters:

   - Design your scripts to accept input parameters that determine the behavior of the script. Parameters could include cell references, ranges, criteria, or any other values that might change.

4. Create Reusable Functions:

   - Package common functionality into reusable functions. Functions make your code modular and allow you to call them with different parameters as needed.

5. Implement Error Handling:

   - Include robust error-handling mechanisms to anticipate potential issues. This ensures that the script gracefully handles errors and provides meaningful feedback.

6. Add User Interaction (Optional):

- Consider incorporating user interfaces, such as input boxes or custom forms, to allow users to provide input or make choices during script execution. This enhances user interaction and makes the script more versatile.

7. Document Your Code:

- Include comments in your code to explain the purpose of each section and the role of variables and parameters. This documentation will help you and others understand the code later.

8. Example: Customizable Data Entry Script:

- Here's a simplified example of a customizable script for data entry that allows users to input data into specified cells:

```vba
Sub CustomizableDataEntry(ByVal inputData As Variant, ByVal targetCell As Range)
        ' Customizable data entry script
        On Error Resume Next ' Enable error handling

        ' Check if the target cell is not locked
        If targetCell.Locked Then
            MsgBox "Target cell is locked. Unable to enter data.", vbExclamation
            Exit Sub
        End If

        ' Input data into the target cell
        targetCell.Value = inputData

        ' Check for errors
        If Err.Number <> 0 Then
```

```
        MsgBox "An error occurred: " & Err.Description,
vbExclamation
    Else
        MsgBox "Data entered successfully!", vbInformation
    End If

    On Error GoTo 0 ' Disable error handling
End Sub
```

9. How to Use the Script:

   - To use this script, you would call it from another procedure or the Immediate Window in the VBA editor, providing the data to input and the target cell as parameters.

```
Sub ExampleUsage()
    Dim dataToEnter As Variant
    Dim targetCell As Range

    ' Set the data to enter and the target cell
    dataToEnter = InputBox("Enter data:")
    Set targetCell = Range("A1") ' Customize the target cell
as needed

    ' Call the customizable data entry script
    CustomizableDataEntry dataToEnter, targetCell
End Sub
```

This example is simplified, but the principles apply to more complex data entry tasks. The key is to design your scripts with flexibility in mind, allowing users to customize inputs and adapt the behavior of the script to various scenarios.

Potential pitfalls and best practices for data automation

Automating data processes using tools like VBA comes with its benefits, but there are potential pitfalls to be aware of. Here are some common pitfalls and best practices for data automation:

Potential pitfalls

1. Lack of Error Handling:

   - Pitfall: Failing to include robust error-handling mechanisms.

   - Best Practice: Implement thorough error handling to anticipate and manage potential issues, preventing unexpected errors from causing script failures.

2. Insufficient Testing:

   - Pitfall: Neglecting thorough testing of automated scripts.

   - Best Practice: Test scripts in various scenarios, including edge cases, to ensure they handle all situations correctly. Regularly review and update scripts as needed.

3. Hard-Coding Values:

   - Pitfall: Hard-coding values into scripts, making them less adaptable.

   - Best Practice: Use parameters, variables, or configuration files to make scripts flexible and easily adjustable to different scenarios without modifying the code.

4. Limited Documentation:

   - Pitfall: Inadequate documentation of scripts and processes.

   - Best Practice: Document the purpose, usage, and variables of your scripts. Clear documentation ensures that others (or yourself in the future) can understand and maintain the code.

5. No Version Control:

   - Pitfall: Not using version control for scripts.

   - Best Practice: Implement version control for your scripts. This ensures that changes can be tracked, rolled back, and collaborated on effectively.

6. Ignoring Security Concerns:

   - Pitfall: Overlooking security considerations, especially when dealing with sensitive data.

   - Best Practice: Implement secure coding practices, protect sensitive information, and adhere to data privacy and security standards.

7. Not Considering Scalability:

   - Pitfall: Developing scripts that don't scale well with increasing data volumes.

   - Best Practice: Design scripts with scalability in mind. Consider potential increases in data size and ensure scripts can handle larger datasets efficiently.

8. Overly Complex Code:

   - Pitfall: Writing overly complex code that is difficult to understand and maintain.

   - Best Practice: Keep code modular, follow best coding practices, and aim for simplicity. Make code easy to read, understand, and modify.

Best practices

1. Modular Design:

   - Best Practice: Design scripts in a modular fashion with well-defined functions or subroutines. This promotes reusability and maintainability.

2. Input Validation:

   - Best Practice: Implement input validation to ensure that the script receives the correct type and format of data.

3. Regular Backups:

   - Best Practice: Regularly backup your data and scripts. This helps mitigate risks in case of unexpected failures or data corruption.

4. Regular Audits:

   - Best Practice: Conduct regular audits of your automated processes to identify any issues, check for accuracy, and ensure compliance with data governance policies.

5. User Training:

   - Best Practice: Provide training for users who will interact with or manage automated processes. Ensure they understand how the automation works and how to troubleshoot common issues.

6. Version Control:

   - Best Practice: Use version control systems like Git to track changes to your scripts. This facilitates collaboration and provides a history of modifications.

7. Monitoring and Logging:

   - Best Practice: Implement monitoring and logging mechanisms to track the performance and behavior of your automated processes. This aids in identifying and resolving issues quickly.

8. Secure Coding Practices:

- Best Practice: Follow secure coding practices to protect against potential security vulnerabilities. Avoid hard-coding sensitive information, and use encryption when necessary.

9. Scalability Considerations:

- Best Practice: Design scripts with scalability in mind. Evaluate the potential impact of increased data volumes and ensure scripts can handle larger datasets efficiently.

10. Regular Review:

- Best Practice: Periodically review and update your scripts. Technologies evolve, and business requirements change, so scripts should be adjusted accordingly.

By being aware of potential pitfalls and following best practices, you can enhance the reliability, security, and maintainability of your automated data processes. Regular reviews and improvements contribute to the long-term success of your automation efforts.

Chapter 3: Financial formulae: VBA for complex calculations

The complexities of financial calculations in Excel

Financial calculations in Excel can involve various complexities, especially when dealing with sophisticated financial models, complex financial instruments, or large datasets. Here are some key complexities associated with financial calculations in Excel:

1. Time Value of Money (TVM):

   - Financial calculations often involve TVM concepts, such as present value, future value, and net present value. Formulas like `PV()`, `FV()`, and `NPV()` can become complex when dealing with irregular cash flows or varying interest rates.

2. Interest rates and compounding:

   - Calculating interest, especially in scenarios with compounding, requires careful consideration. The use of nominal and effective interest rates, different compounding frequencies, and handling inflation can introduce complexities.

3. Loan amortization:

   - Calculating loan amortization schedules involves intricate formulas, such as the PMT() function, which considers interest, principal repayments, and the timing of cash flows. Handling changes in interest rates or extra payments can add further complexity.

4. Risk and return analysis:

- Analyzing risk and return often involves statistical calculations, such as standard deviation and beta. These calculations can be complex and may require additional tools or add-ins.

5. Option pricing models:

- Valuing financial options (e.g., Black-Scholes model) involves complex mathematical formulas. Implementing these models in Excel can be challenging due to the involvement of statistical functions and iterative calculations.

6. Cash flow analysis:

- Analyzing cash flows in financial models requires handling multiple cash flow streams, discounting, and adjusting for tax considerations. Large-scale cash flow models can become intricate, requiring careful organization and referencing.

7. Macroeconomic factors:

- Financial models often incorporate macroeconomic factors like inflation rates, GDP growth, and interest rate changes. Linking these factors to financial projections adds complexity, especially when considering the impact of external variables.

8. Financial statements modeling:

- Building financial statements (income statement, balance sheet, and cash flow statement) involves linking various accounts, applying accounting principles, and ensuring that the statements balance. Changes in assumptions or business conditions can complicate modeling.

9. Scenario analysis and sensitivity analysis:

- Assessing the impact of different scenarios and performing sensitivity analysis involves creating multiple versions of a financial model. Managing and comparing these scenarios can become complex as the number of variables increases.

10. Currency exchange and translation:

- Working with multiple currencies introduces complexities related to exchange rates and translation. Formulas like `XLOOKUP()` or `VLOOKUP()` may be used to fetch exchange rates and convert values.

11. Data validation and quality:

- Ensuring the accuracy and reliability of data is critical. Validating data sources, cleaning data, and handling outliers or missing values are important aspects of building robust financial models.

12. Regulatory compliance:

- Complying with regulatory requirements may involve complex calculations and reporting standards. Staying current with changes in regulations and adjusting models accordingly is essential.

13. Integration with external data sources:

- Importing and integrating data from external sources, such as financial databases or APIs, may introduce complexities related to data formatting, consistency, and handling frequent updates.

To navigate these complexities, financial modelers often rely on a combination of Excel functions, advanced modeling techniques, and, in some cases, the use of specialized financial modeling software. Regular auditing, documentation, and validation checks are crucial for maintaining the accuracy and reliability of financial models. It's also important to stay informed about changes in financial accounting standards and regulations that may impact calculations.

The application of VBA in automating intricate financial formulas

Certainly! Below are a few examples demonstrating the application of VBA in automating intricate financial formulas. In these examples, VBA is used to perform calculations related to loan amortization, present value, and future value.

1. Loan Amortization Schedule:

- Objective: Create a VBA script to generate a loan amortization schedule.

```vba
Sub GenerateAmortizationSchedule()
    Dim principal As Double
    Dim interestRate As Double
    Dim loanTerm As Integer
    Dim monthlyPayment As Double

    ' Input parameters
    principal = InputBox("Enter loan amount:")
    interestRate = InputBox("Enter annual interest rate:")
    loanTerm = InputBox("Enter loan term in years:")

    ' Calculate monthly payment using the PMT function
    monthlyPayment = WorksheetFunction.Pmt(interestRate / 12,
loanTerm * 12, -principal)

    ' Create headers in a new sheet
    Sheets.Add(After:=Sheets(Sheets.Count)).Name =
"Amortization Schedule"
    Sheets("Amortization Schedule").Range("A1").Value =
"Payment Number"
    Sheets("Amortization Schedule").Range("B1").Value =
"Payment Amount"
    Sheets("Amortization Schedule").Range("C1").Value =
"Principal Payment"
```

```vba
        Sheets("Amortization Schedule").Range("D1").Value =
"Interest Payment"
        Sheets("Amortization Schedule").Range("E1").Value =
"Remaining Balance"

        ' Generate amortization schedule
        Dim remainingBalance As Double
        remainingBalance = principal

        For i = 1 To loanTerm * 12
            ' Calculate interest and principal payments
            Dim interestPayment As Double
            Dim principalPayment As Double
            interestPayment = remainingBalance * interestRate / 12
            principalPayment = monthlyPayment - interestPayment

            ' Update remaining balance
            remainingBalance = remainingBalance - principalPayment

            ' Populate the schedule
            Sheets("Amortization Schedule").Cells(i + 1, 1).Value =
i
            Sheets("Amortization Schedule").Cells(i + 1, 2).Value =
monthlyPayment
            Sheets("Amortization Schedule").Cells(i + 1, 3).Value =
principalPayment
            Sheets("Amortization Schedule").Cells(i + 1, 4).Value =
interestPayment
            Sheets("Amortization Schedule").Cells(i + 1, 5).Value =
remainingBalance
        Next i
    End Sub
```

2. Present Value (PV) Calculation:

- Objective: Create a VBA script to calculate the present value of future cash flows.

```
Function CalculatePV(rate As Double, nper As Double, pmt As
Double, futureValue As Double) As Double
    ' Calculate Present Value using the PV function
    CalculatePV = WorksheetFunction.PV(rate, nper, pmt,
futureValue)
    End Function
```

- To use this function in a worksheet, you can enter a formula like **=CalculatePV(0.05, 10, -500, 0)** to calculate the present value.

3. Future Value (FV) calculation:

- Objective: Create a VBA script to calculate the future value of an investment.

```
Function CalculateFV(rate As Double, nper As Double, pmt As
Double, presentValue As Double) As Double
    ' Calculate Future Value using the FV function
    CalculateFV = WorksheetFunction.FV(rate, nper, pmt,
presentValue)
    End Function
```

- To use this function in a worksheet, you can enter a formula like `=CalculateFV(0.05, 10, -500, 0)` to calculate the future value.

These examples illustrate how VBA can be used to automate financial calculations by creating custom functions or scripts that leverage Excel's built-in financial functions. VBA enables customization, automation, and the integration of financial calculations into more comprehensive applications or models.

Ready-to-use scripts for common financial calculations

Below are ready-to-use VBA scripts for common financial calculations. These scripts can be copied and pasted into the VBA editor in Excel to perform calculations related to present value, future value, loan payments, and interest rates.

1. Present Value (PV) Calculation:

 - This script calculates the present value of future cash flows using the PV function.

```
Function CalculatePV(rate As Double, nper As Double, pmt As
Double, futureValue As Double) As Double
    ' Calculate Present Value using the PV function
    CalculatePV = WorksheetFunction.PV(rate, nper, pmt,
futureValue)
    End Function
```

2. Future Value (FV) Calculation:

 - This script calculates the future value of an investment using the FV function.

```
Function CalculateFV(rate As Double, nper As Double, pmt As
Double, presentValue As Double) As Double
    ' Calculate Future Value using the FV function
    CalculateFV = WorksheetFunction.FV(rate, nper, pmt,
presentValue)
    End Function
```

3. Loan Payment Calculation:

- This script calculates the periodic payment for a loan using the PMT function.

```
Function CalculateLoanPayment(rate As Double, nper As Double,
presentValue As Double) As Double
    ' Calculate Loan Payment using the PMT function
    CalculateLoanPayment = WorksheetFunction.PMT(rate, nper, -
presentValue)
End Function
```

4. Interest Rate Calculation:

- This script calculates the interest rate for a loan using the RATE function.

```
Function CalculateInterestRate(nper As Double, pmt As Double,
presentValue As Double, futureValue As Double) As Double
    ' Calculate Interest Rate using the RATE function
    CalculateInterestRate = WorksheetFunction.RATE(nper, pmt,
presentValue, futureValue)
End Function
```

How to use these scripts:

1. Open Excel:

- Open your Excel workbook.

2. Access the VBA Editor:

- Press `Alt + F11` to open the VBA editor.

3. Insert a Module:

- Right-click on any item in the Project Explorer, select "Insert," and then choose "Module."

4. Copy and Paste the Script:

- Copy the desired script above and paste it into the module in the VBA editor.

5. Use the Function in Excel:

- Go back to your Excel workbook, and you can now use these functions like any other Excel function. For example, you can enter a formula like `=CalculatePV(0.05, 10, -500, 0)` in a cell to calculate the present value.

These scripts provide ready-to-use functions for common financial calculations, making it easy to incorporate them into your financial models or Excel worksheets.

Tips for optimizing and customizing financial scripts

Certainly! Optimizing and customizing financial scripts is crucial for ensuring efficiency, accuracy, and flexibility in your Excel-based financial models. Here are some tips to help you achieve that:

1. Use constants for parameters:

- Replace hardcoded values in your scripts with named constants. This makes it easier to customize and adjust parameters without modifying the code directly.

```
' Instead of:
Function CalculatePV(rate As Double, nper As Double, pmt As Double, futureValue As Double) As Double

' Use:
```

```
Function CalculatePV(rate As Double, nper As Double, pmt As
Double, futureValue As Double) As Double
        Const MONTHLY_RATE As Double = 1 / 12
        ' ... rest of the function ...
```

2. Parameterize inputs:

- Allow users to input parameters through custom interfaces, such as input boxes or user forms. This enhances user experience and allows for dynamic customization.

```
Sub UserInputExample()
        Dim rate As Double
        Dim nper As Double
        Dim pmt As Double
        Dim futureValue As Double

        ' Get user inputs
        rate = InputBox("Enter interest rate:")
        nper = InputBox("Enter number of periods:")
        pmt = InputBox("Enter payment amount:")
        futureValue = InputBox("Enter future value:")

        ' Call the calculation function
        Dim result As Double
        result = CalculatePV(rate, nper, pmt, futureValue)
        MsgBox "Present Value: " & result
    End Sub
```

3. Error handling:

- Implement robust error-handling routines to catch and address potential issues. This ensures the reliability of your scripts, especially when dealing with user inputs or external data.

```
Function CalculatePV(rate As Double, nper As Double, pmt As
Double, futureValue As Double) As Double
     On Error Resume Next
     CalculatePV = WorksheetFunction.PV(rate, nper, pmt,
futureValue)
     If Err.Number <> 0 Then
          MsgBox "An error occurred: " & Err.Description,
vbExclamation
     End If
     On Error GoTo 0
   End Function
```

4. Avoid volatile functions:

- Minimize the use of volatile functions (functions that recalculate every time any change occurs in the worksheet), as they can impact performance. Instead, use non-volatile alternatives where possible.

5. Use array formulas wisely:

- If working with large datasets, consider using array formulas for efficiency. However, be mindful of the increased calculation load on the worksheet.

6. Implement caching:

- For repeated calculations with the same inputs, consider implementing caching mechanisms to store and reuse results. This can significantly improve performance.

7. Optimize iterative calculations:

- If your financial model involves iterative calculations, optimize the iteration process. Use iteration settings in Excel, and ensure that your scripts handle convergence and divergence efficiently.

8. Dynamic range references:

- Use dynamic named ranges to refer to data ranges dynamically. This ensures that your scripts adapt to changes in the size of datasets.

9. Document your code:

- Include comments and documentation within your code. Clearly explain the purpose of each section, the role of variables, and any assumptions made. This helps both yourself and others who may work with the code.

10. Regularly review and optimize:

- Periodically review your scripts for optimization opportunities. As data volumes or model complexity increase, adjustments may be needed for continued efficiency.

11. Understand Excel's calculation engine:

- Familiarize yourself with how Excel's calculation engine works. Understand the order of operations and how Excel recalculates formulas.

> Understanding the order of operations and how Excel recalculates formulas is essential for creating accurate and efficient worksheets. The order of operations in Excel is governed by a set of rules that determine the sequence in which formulas are evaluated. Here is an overview of the key principles:
>
> Order of operations in Excel:
>
> 1. Parentheses:
>
> - Excel follows the standard mathematical rule of performing operations inside parentheses first. If a formula contains parentheses, the expressions within them are calculated before anything else.
>
> 2. Exponents:

- After parentheses, Excel calculates any exponentiation operations. For example, if a formula includes powers or roots (e.g., ^ or SQRT), these operations are performed next.

3. Multiplication and Division:

- Multiplication (*) and division (/) operations are performed from left to right. If there are multiple multiplication or division operations in a formula, Excel evaluates them in the order they appear.

4. Addition and Subtraction:

- Finally, addition (+) and subtraction (-) operations are performed from left to right. Similar to multiplication and division, Excel follows the order in which these operations appear in the formula.

Excel recalculation process:

Excel employs a recalculation process to update the values in cells based on changes to the data or formulas. The recalculation process occurs automatically and involves the following steps:

1. Dependency tree:

- Excel builds a dependency tree or calculation chain to identify the relationships between cells. It determines which cells depend on the value of other cells.

2. Dirty cells:

- Excel identifies "dirty" cells, which are cells that have changed or depend on changed cells. These cells need recalculation.

3. Recalculation order:

- Excel determines the order in which formulas should be recalculated based on the dependency tree. It starts with the cells that have changed and recalculates formulas in a logical sequence.

4. Iterative Calculation (if enabled):

- If iterative calculation is enabled in Excel settings, the recalculation process may involve multiple iterations to converge on a solution for cells with circular references or iterative formulas.

5. Update values:

- Excel updates the values in the cells based on the recalculated formulas.

6. Events and triggers:

- Certain events or triggers, such as manual recalculation, opening the workbook, or changes in external data sources, can initiate the recalculation process.

Tips for optimizing recalculation:

1. Minimize Volatile Functions:

- Volatile functions, such as `NOW()`, `TODAY()`, and `RAND()`, recalculate whenever any change occurs in the worksheet. Minimize their use to improve performance.

2. Use Manual Recalculation:

- Switching to manual recalculation (`Formulas > Calculation Options > Manual`) can be useful in large worksheets. You can then recalculate manually when needed.

3. Optimize Formulas:

- Simplify and optimize complex formulas to reduce calculation time. Break down large formulas into smaller parts if possible.

4. Use Array Formulas Wisely:

- Array formulas can be powerful but may slow down recalculation. Use them judiciously, especially with large datasets.

5. Disable Iterative Calculation if Unnecessary:

- If your workbook doesn't involve iterative calculations, consider disabling iterative calculation (`**File > Options > Formulas > Enable iterative calculation**`) to improve performance.

6. Check for Circular References:

- Circular references can lead to inefficiencies. Resolve any circular references in your workbook.

Understanding the order of operations and the recalculation process in Excel allows you to create more efficient and reliable worksheets, especially in the context of financial modeling and complex calculations.

12. Profile Your Code:

- Use profiling tools to identify bottlenecks in your code. This can help you pinpoint areas that need optimization.

By following these tips, you can create financial scripts that are not only accurate but also customizable, user-friendly, and efficient. Regularly revisiting and refining your scripts ensures that they remain optimized as your financial models evolve.

Chapter 4: Beyond worksheets: Automating reporting

The limitations of manual reporting in Excel

While Excel is a powerful tool for data analysis and reporting, there are limitations to manual reporting that users should be aware of. Here are some common limitations:

1. Manual data entry errors:

   - Human error is a significant risk in manual reporting. Typos, incorrect data entry, and formula mistakes can lead to inaccurate results.

2. Time-consuming:

   - Manual reporting can be time-consuming, especially when dealing with large datasets or complex calculations. Users may spend a significant amount of time inputting, organizing, and validating data.

3. Version control challenges:

   - Maintaining version control is challenging in manual reporting. As data and reports evolve, it becomes difficult to track changes and ensure that everyone is working with the latest information.

4. Limited scalability:

   - As data volumes and reporting requirements grow, manual reporting becomes less scalable. Excel may struggle to handle large datasets efficiently, leading to performance issues.

5. Lack of automation:

- Manual reporting lacks automation, requiring users to perform repetitive tasks. Automation is crucial for efficiency and reducing the risk of errors.

6. Data security concerns:

- Excel files may not provide robust security features, making them susceptible to unauthorized access or data breaches. Protecting sensitive information can be challenging.

7. Limited collaboration:

- Collaborating on Excel files can be challenging, especially when multiple users need to work on the same file simultaneously. This can result in conflicts, and version control becomes more difficult.

8. Difficulty in handling large datasets:

- Excel has limitations in handling very large datasets. Users may experience performance issues, and tasks like sorting, filtering, and calculations may slow down.

9. Limited data visualization options:

- Excel offers basic data visualization tools, but for advanced and interactive visualizations, users may need to export data to specialized tools. This can disrupt the reporting workflow.

10. Lack of data validation:

- Ensuring data accuracy and consistency can be challenging in manual reporting. Excel does provide validation features, but enforcing complex validation rules may require additional effort.

11. Formula complexity and error handling:

- Managing complex formulas and error handling can be challenging. Users may encounter difficulties in tracking errors, and complex formulas may make the spreadsheet less transparent.

12. Dependency on individual skills:

- Manual reporting relies heavily on the skills and expertise of individual users. If key personnel are unavailable or lack specific skills, it can impact the reporting process.

13. Limited audit trail:

- Tracking changes and creating an audit trail is limited in Excel. It may be difficult to trace the origin of data or understand the sequence of changes.

14. Risk of data redundancy:

- In a manual reporting environment, data redundancy is a risk. Multiple copies of the same data may exist in different files, increasing the chance of inconsistencies.

15. Difficulty in handling unstructured data:

- Excel is more structured, and handling unstructured data (text, images, etc.) may require additional tools or manual processing.

To address these limitations, organizations often turn to Business Intelligence (BI) tools, data visualization platforms, or custom applications that provide automation, collaboration features, advanced security, and scalability beyond what Excel can offer.

The concept of dynamic and automated reporting through VBA

Dynamic and automated reporting through VBA (Visual Basic for Applications) in Excel involves creating scripts that can manipulate and update data, generate reports, and perform various tasks automatically. This is particularly useful when dealing with large datasets, complex calculations, or when regular and repetitive reporting is required. Here's an overview of the concepts and steps involved:

Dynamic reporting with VBA:

1. Dynamic named ranges:

   - Use dynamic named ranges in Excel to create flexible references that adjust automatically as the underlying data changes. VBA can be used to dynamically update these ranges based on the size of the dataset.

```
' Example: Dynamic named range for a column of data
Sub CreateDynamicRange()
    Dim LastRow As Long
    LastRow = Cells(Rows.Count, "A").End(xlUp).Row
    ThisWorkbook.Names.Add Name:="DynamicRange",
RefersTo:=Range("A2:A" & LastRow)
End Sub
```

2. Data validation and input forms:

   - Implement data validation and input forms using VBA to ensure that users enter accurate and consistent data. This enhances the reliability of your reports.

```
' Example: Data validation for a cell
Sub SetDataValidation()
```

```
With Range("A1").Validation
    .Delete
    .Add Type:=xlValidateWholeNumber,
AlertStyle:=xlValidAlertStop, Operator:= _
        xlBetween, Formula1:="1", Formula2:="100"
    .IgnoreBlank = True
    .InCellDropdown = True
    .ShowInput = True
    .ShowError = True
End With
End Sub
```

Automated reporting with VBA:

1. Automate Calculations:

- Use VBA to automate complex calculations. This is useful when dealing with financial models, projections, or any scenario requiring iterative calculations.

```
' Example: Automated calculation using VBA
Sub CalculateData()
    ' Your calculation logic here
    Range("B1").Value = Range("A1").Value * 2
End Sub
```

2. Report generation:

- Create VBA scripts to automate the generation of reports. This can involve pulling data from databases, performing calculations, and populating predefined templates.

```
' Example: Automated report generation
Sub GenerateReport()
    ' Your report generation logic here
```

```
    ' Copy data from a database, perform calculations, and
populate a template
    End Sub
```

3. Automate data import:

- Use VBA to automate the import of data from external sources, such as databases, CSV files, or APIs. This ensures that your reports are always based on the latest data.

```
    ' Example: Automated data import from a CSV file
    Sub ImportData()
        With
ActiveSheet.QueryTables.Add(Connection:="TEXT;C:\Path\To\Your\File
.csv", _
            Destination:=Range("A1"))
            .TextFileParseType = xlDelimited
            .Refresh
        End With
    End Sub
```

4. Scheduled tasks with Windows Task Scheduler:

- Combine VBA with Windows Task Scheduler to automate reports at scheduled intervals. This is particularly useful for generating daily, weekly, or monthly reports.

5. Automate Email Distribution:

- Use VBA to automate the distribution of reports via email. Attach generated reports to emails and send them to predefined recipients.

```
    ' Example: Automated email distribution
    Sub SendEmail()
        ' Your email sending logic here
```

```
    ' Attach the generated report and send it to recipients
End Sub
```

6. User-friendly interfaces:

 - Design user-friendly interfaces using VBA UserForms to allow users to interact with and customize reports before generation.

```
    ' Example: UserForm for report customization
Sub ShowReportOptions()
        ' Your UserForm logic here
        ' Allow users to customize report parameters
End Sub
```

By combining dynamic named ranges, data validation, automated calculations, and report generation using VBA, you can create powerful, flexible, and automated reporting systems in Excel. These scripts enhance efficiency, reduce errors, and allow users to focus on analysis rather than manual tasks.

Sample scripts for generating customizable reports

Below are sample VBA scripts for generating customizable reports in Excel. These scripts demonstrate how to create user-friendly interfaces using UserForms to allow users to customize report parameters before generating the reports.

 1. UserForm for report customization:

```
' Open a UserForm for report customization
Sub ShowReportOptions()
    UserForm1.Show
End Sub
```

2. UserForm code for report customization:

This script assumes you have a UserForm named "UserForm1" with relevant controls such as TextBoxes, ComboBoxes, and Buttons. The UserForm allows users to input parameters for the report.

```
Private Sub OKButton_Click()
    ' Retrieve user inputs from the UserForm
    Dim startDate As Date
    Dim endDate As Date
    Dim category As String

    startDate = DateValue(Me.StartDateTextBox.Value)
    endDate = DateValue(Me.EndDateTextBox.Value)
    category = Me.CategoryComboBox.Value

    ' Call the function to generate the report with the selected
parameters
    GenerateReport startDate, endDate, category

    ' Close the UserForm
    Unload Me
End Sub

Private Sub CancelButton_Click()
    ' Close the UserForm without generating the report
    Unload Me
End Sub
```

3. Report Generation Function:

This script assumes you have a function named "GenerateReport" that accepts parameters for customization. Customize this function based on your specific reporting needs.

```
Sub GenerateReport(startDate As Date, endDate As Date, category As
String)
    ' Your report generation logic here
    ' Use the provided parameters to filter data and generate the
report

    ' For demonstration purposes, let's display a message
    MsgBox "Generating report for Category: " & category & vbCrLf
& _
            "Start Date: " & Format(startDate, "Short Date") &
vbCrLf & _
            "End Date: " & Format(endDate, "Short Date"),
vbInformation
End Sub
```

How to set up and use the scripts:

1. Create a UserForm:

   - In the Excel VBA editor, insert a UserForm (Insert > UserForm). Add controls such as TextBoxes, ComboBoxes, and Buttons for users to input customization parameters.

2. Copy and paste code:

   - Copy the code for the UserForm and the Report Generation Function into the respective code windows in the VBA editor.

3. Run the ShowReportOptions Macro:

   - Create a new module and paste the code for the `ShowReportOptions` macro. Run this macro to display the UserForm.

84

4. Customize and generate report:

- Users can input parameters in the UserForm, click the OK button to generate the report based on the selected parameters, or click Cancel to close the UserForm without generating the report.

This example provides a basic structure for creating customizable reports using a UserForm. Depending on your reporting requirements, you can enhance the UserForm, modify the parameters passed to the `GenerateReport` function, and extend the report generation logic accordingly.

Strategies for personalizing reports based on specific accounting needs

Personalizing reports based on specific accounting needs involves tailoring financial reports to meet the unique requirements of a business or individual. Here are strategies for achieving personalized accounting reports:

1. Understand stakeholder requirements:

- Engage with stakeholders, including management, accountants, and decision-makers, to understand their specific reporting needs. Clarify the purpose of the reports, the information they require, and the frequency of reporting.

2. Customizable report templates:

- Create customizable report templates that allow users to select and arrange key financial metrics based on their preferences. Use Excel features like PivotTables, slicers, and dynamic named ranges to enable easy customization.

3. Parameterized reports:

- Implement parameterized reports that allow users to input specific criteria such as date ranges, departments, or product categories. Use VBA scripts to prompt users for parameters and dynamically adjust report content accordingly

4. Automated data import and integration:

- Automate the import of data from various sources, such as accounting software, databases, or external files. Ensure seamless integration to provide real-time or near-real-time updates in reports.

5. Dynamic named ranges:

- Utilize dynamic named ranges in Excel to automatically adjust the range of data included in reports as new transactions or data points are added. This ensures that reports always reflect the most up-to-date information.

6. Interactive dashboards:

- Create interactive dashboards that allow users to drill down into specific details. Use charts, graphs, and slicers to enhance visualization and provide a comprehensive view of financial data.

7. Role-based access:

- Implement role-based access controls to restrict access to sensitive financial information. Tailor reports based on user roles, ensuring that individuals only have access to data relevant to their responsibilities.

8. Consolidated reporting:

- For businesses with multiple departments or subsidiaries, implement consolidated reporting features. Create summary reports that roll up information from various entities while still providing the ability to view detailed reports for each entity.

9. Alerts and notifications:

- Integrate alerts and notifications into reports to highlight key financial metrics or notify stakeholders of exceptions or important events. This ensures timely attention to critical financial information.

10. Mobile-friendly reports:

- Design reports that are mobile-friendly, allowing stakeholders to access key financial information on the go. Consider responsive design principles for usability on various devices.

11. Trend analysis and forecasting:

- Include trend analysis and forecasting tools in reports to help stakeholders understand historical performance and make informed decisions about the future.

12. Audit trail and versioning:

- Incorporate features such as audit trails and versioning to track changes made to reports over time. This provides transparency and accountability in financial reporting.

13. Documentation and training:

- Provide documentation and training resources for users to understand how to personalize and interpret reports effectively. Ensure that users are aware of the available features and customization options.

14. Regular feedback and iterative improvement:

- Solicit feedback from users on the effectiveness of reports and continuously iterate on the design based on evolving business needs. Regularly assess the relevance and usability of reports.

15. Compliance and regulatory considerations:

- Ensure that personalized reports comply with accounting standards and regulatory requirements. Customizations should not compromise accuracy, consistency, or compliance.

By implementing these strategies, businesses can create personalized accounting reports that align with specific needs, preferences, and workflows, fostering better decision-making and financial management.

Chapter 5: Error-proof accounting: VBA for accuracy

The common errors in manual accounting processes

Manual accounting processes are susceptible to various errors that can impact the accuracy and reliability of financial information. Here are some common errors associated with manual accounting:

1. Data entry errors:

   - Typographical Errors: Typos in numbers, account names, or descriptions can lead to inaccurate data.

   - Transposition Errors: Mistakes in the order of digits, such as entering "54" instead of "45," can result in significant miscalculations.

2. Calculation errors:

   - Mathematical Mistakes: Errors in addition, subtraction, multiplication, or division can occur during manual calculations.

   - Formula Errors: Mistakes in using formulas or applying them inconsistently across entries can lead to incorrect results.

3. Posting errors:

   - Posting to Wrong Accounts: Misplacing entries in incorrect ledger accounts can distort financial statements.

- Duplicate Postings: Accidentally posting the same transaction more than once can lead to overstatement of revenues or expenses.

4. Reconciliation errors:

- Bank Reconciliation Mistakes: Failing to reconcile bank statements with the general ledger can result in discrepancies.

- Supplier and Customer Reconciliation Errors: Misalignments in accounts payable and accounts receivable can lead to misunderstandings with suppliers or customers.

5. Classification errors:

- Misclassification of Expenses or Revenues: Assigning transactions to incorrect expense or revenue categories can distort financial reporting.

- Failure to Segregate Accounts: Mixing personal and business transactions can lead to confusion and errors.

6. Timing errors:

- Recording Transactions in the Wrong Period: Failing to record transactions in the correct accounting period can affect financial statement accuracy.

- Failure to Accrue or Defer: Not recognizing expenses or revenues in the appropriate period can lead to inaccuracies.

7. Missing transactions:

- Omission of Transactions: Overlooking certain transactions or failing to record them can result in incomplete financial records.

8. Incomplete documentation:

- Lack of Supporting Documentation: Insufficient documentation for transactions can make it challenging to trace and verify entries.

9. Currency conversion errors:

- Errors in Currency Conversions: For businesses dealing with multiple currencies, miscalculations in currency conversions can impact financial reporting.

10. Communication errors:

- Miscommunication Between Departments: Lack of clear communication between departments or individuals involved in the accounting process can lead to errors.

11. Manual process vulnerabilities:

- Limited Internal Controls: Manual processes may lack robust internal controls, increasing the risk of errors and fraud.

- Dependency on Individuals: Relying on specific individuals for key accounting tasks can be risky if there is a lack of redundancy or oversight.

12. Overreliance on spreadsheets:

- Excel Formula Errors: Mistakes in complex Excel formulas or lack of understanding of spreadsheet functions can result in errors.

13. Failure to update chart of accounts:

- Outdated Chart of Accounts: Failing to update the chart of accounts to reflect changes in the business structure or operations can lead to misclassification.

14. Human errors:

- Fatigue and Distraction: Human factors, such as fatigue or distraction, can contribute to errors in manual accounting processes.

15. Failure to adhere to accounting standards:

- Non-compliance with Standards: Failing to adhere to accounting standards and principles can result in errors and misrepresentations in financial statements.

To mitigate these errors, businesses often turn to automated accounting systems, which can provide checks and balances, reduce manual data entry, and enhance overall accuracy in financial reporting. Regular training, implementing internal controls, and conducting periodic audits are also effective strategies to minimize errors in manual accounting processes.

How VBA scripts can enhance accuracy and minimize errors?

VBA (Visual Basic for Applications) scripts can enhance accuracy and minimize errors in several ways within Excel and other Microsoft Office applications. Here are ways in which VBA scripts contribute to accuracy:

1. Automation of repetitive tasks:

  - Issue: Manual errors can occur in repetitive tasks.

  - VBA Solution: Automate repetitive tasks, such as data entry, calculations, or formatting, reducing the chances of human error associated with manual execution.

2. Data validation and input checks:

  - Issue: Incorrect data entry can lead to errors.

  - VBA Solution: Implement data validation checks in VBA scripts to ensure that entered data meets specified criteria, reducing the likelihood of invalid entries.

3. Dynamic named ranges:

   - Issue: Static ranges may lead to inaccurate calculations if data size changes.

   - VBA Solution: Use VBA to create dynamic named ranges that automatically adjust based on the size of the dataset, ensuring accurate calculations.

4. Error handling and logging:

   - Issue: Errors during script execution may go unnoticed.

   - VBA Solution: Implement robust error handling in VBA scripts to catch and handle errors gracefully. Log error details for analysis and troubleshooting.

5. Consistency in formatting:

   - Issue: Inconsistent formatting may impact data interpretation.

   - VBA Solution: Use VBA to enforce consistent formatting rules across worksheets, ensuring that data is presented uniformly.

6. Data cleaning and transformation:

   - Issue: Raw data may contain errors or inconsistencies.

   - VBA Solution: Write scripts to clean and transform data, addressing issues like missing values, outliers, or inconsistent formats.

7. Automated data validation:

   - Issue: Manually validating large datasets is time-consuming and error-prone.

   - VBA Solution: Develop scripts to automate data validation processes, checking for anomalies, duplicates, or outliers.

8. Automated report generation:

   - Issue: Manual report creation may lead to errors and delays.

- VBA Solution: Use VBA scripts to automate report generation, pulling data, performing calculations, and creating formatted reports with minimal human intervention.

9. Enhanced user interfaces:

   - Issue: Users may struggle with complex or error-prone interfaces.

   - VBA Solution: Design user-friendly interfaces using VBA UserForms to guide users through processes, reducing the likelihood of errors.

10. Integration with external systems:

   - Issue: Manually entering data from external sources may introduce errors.

   - VBA Solution: Develop scripts to automatically import data from external systems, reducing the risk of transcription errors.

11. Calculation accuracy:

   - Issue: Manual calculations may introduce errors.

   - VBA Solution: Write VBA scripts to perform complex calculations with precision, reducing the likelihood of calculation errors.

12. Automated data backups:

   - Issue: Loss of data due to accidental deletion or system failures.

   - VBA Solution: Implement VBA scripts to automatically create backups of critical data, minimizing the impact of data loss.

13. Consistent application of business rules:

   - Issue: Inconsistent application of business rules may lead to discrepancies.

   - VBA Solution: Embed business rules into VBA scripts, ensuring their consistent application across different processes.

14. User guidance and documentation:

   - Issue: Lack of guidance may lead to user errors.

   - VBA Solution: Use VBA to create tooltips, input prompts, or documentation within applications, providing guidance and reducing the likelihood of errors.

15. Regular auditing and logging:

   - Issue: Lack of visibility into changes and actions taken.

   - VBA Solution: Implement logging mechanisms in VBA scripts to record actions, changes, and events, facilitating regular audits.

By leveraging VBA scripts strategically, you can create automated, consistent, and error-resistant processes in Excel and other Microsoft Office applications, significantly enhancing accuracy and reducing the risk of manual errors.

Scripts for error-checking and validation

Certainly! Below are examples of VBA scripts that demonstrate error-checking and validation techniques. These scripts showcase how to implement checks for data validation, handle errors gracefully, and log error details for analysis.

1. Data validation and error handling for user input:

```
Sub ValidateUserInput()
    Dim userInput As Variant

    ' Prompt user for input
    On Error Resume Next
    userInput = InputBox("Enter a number:")
    On Error GoTo 0

    ' Check if input is a valid number
```

```vba
    If IsNumeric(userInput) Then
        ' Process the valid input
        MsgBox "You entered: " & userInput, vbInformation
    Else
        ' Handle invalid input
        MsgBox "Invalid input. Please enter a valid number.",
vbExclamation
    End If
End Sub
```

2. Error handling and logging:

```vba
Sub PerformOperation()
    On Error Resume Next

    ' Perform some operation that may raise an error
    Dim result As Double
    result = 1 / 0 ' This will cause a runtime error

    ' Check for errors
    If Err.Number <> 0 Then
        ' Log error details
        LogError "PerformOperation", Err.Description
        ' Inform the user about the error
        MsgBox "An error occurred: " & Err.Description,
vbExclamation
        ' Clear the error
        Err.Clear
    End If

    On Error GoTo 0
End Sub

Sub LogError(procName As String, errMsg As String)
    ' Log error details to a file or another log system
```

```vba
    Dim logFile As Integer
    Dim logMessage As String
    logFile = FreeFile
    Open "ErrorLog.txt" For Append As logFile
    logMessage = Now & " - Procedure: " & procName & ", Error: " &
errMsg & vbCrLf
    Print #logFile, logMessage
    Close logFile
End Sub
```

3. Data validation and formatting:

```vba
Sub ValidateAndFormatData()
    Dim dataRange As Range
    Dim cell As Range

    ' Assume data is in column A starting from A2
    Set dataRange = Range("A2:A" & Cells(Rows.Count,
"A").End(xlUp).Row)

    For Each cell In dataRange
        ' Check if the data is a valid date
        If IsDate(cell.Value) Then
            ' Format valid dates in a consistent way
            cell.Value = Format(cell.Value, "yyyy-mm-dd")
        Else
            ' Handle invalid dates
            cell.Interior.Color = RGB(255, 0, 0) ' Mark invalid
data with red background
        End If
    Next cell
End Sub
```

4. Check for duplicates and highlight:

```vba
Sub CheckForDuplicates()
    Dim dataRange As Range
    Dim cell As Range
    Dim duplicateCount As Integer

    ' Assume data is in column B starting from B2
    Set dataRange = Range("B2:B" & Cells(Rows.Count,
"B").End(xlUp).Row)

    ' Initialize duplicate count
    duplicateCount = 0

    ' Loop through each cell in the range
    For Each cell In dataRange
        ' Check for duplicates
        If WorksheetFunction.CountIf(dataRange, cell.Value) > 1
Then
            ' Highlight duplicate cells
            cell.Interior.Color = RGB(255, 0, 0) ' Mark duplicates
with red background
            duplicateCount = duplicateCount + 1
        End If
    Next cell

    ' Display the number of duplicates found
    MsgBox duplicateCount & " duplicates found.", vbInformation
End Sub
```

These scripts provide examples of how VBA can be used for data validation, error handling, and logging. Customize the scripts based on your specific requirements and integrate them into your Excel workflows for enhanced accuracy and reliability.

The best practices for maintaining data integrity

Maintaining data integrity is crucial for ensuring the accuracy, consistency, and reliability of information in a database or spreadsheet. Here are some best practices to help you maintain data integrity:

1. Use data validation:

   - Implement data validation rules to restrict the type and range of data that can be entered into cells. This helps prevent errors and ensures that only valid data is input.

2. Enforce referential integrity:

   - In relational databases, enforce referential integrity by using primary and foreign keys This ensures that relationships between tables are maintained, and data remains consistent across related tables.

3. Implement unique constraints:

   - Enforce unique constraints on fields that require unique values, such as primary keys. This prevents the entry of duplicate records and maintains the uniqueness of key identifiers.

4. Regularly update and cleanse data:

   - Periodically update and cleanse data to remove duplicates, correct errors, and standardize formats. This helps maintain the accuracy and consistency of the data over time.

5. Use transactions:

- When working with databases, use transactions to group a set of operations into a single, atomic unit. This ensures that either all operations are completed successfully, or none are, maintaining consistency.

6. Implement data auditing:

- Enable auditing features to track changes to the data. Maintain an audit trail that includes information about who made the changes, what changes were made, and when they occurred.

7. Establish data quality standards:

- Define and document data quality standards to ensure that data is accurate, complete, and meets specific criteria. Establish clear guidelines for data entry and validation.

8. Perform regular backups:

- Regularly back up your data to prevent data loss due to accidental deletion, corruption, or system failures. This ensures that you can restore data to a known, reliable state.

9. Implement access controls:

- Use access controls to restrict user access to sensitive data. Define roles and permissions to ensure that users only have access to the data they need for their responsibilities.

10. Educate users and provide training:

- Educate users about the importance of data integrity and provide training on data entry best practices. This helps reduce errors caused by user misunderstanding or lack of awareness.

11. Standardize data formats:

- Standardize data formats for consistency. Use consistent date formats, units of measurement, and naming conventions to avoid confusion and errors.

12. Use error-checking tools:

- Leverage built-in error-checking tools in spreadsheet applications or database management systems. These tools can help identify potential errors, inconsistencies, or issues with data.

13. Implement data validation checks in code:

- When working with databases or scripts, implement additional data validation checks in code to ensure that data adheres to predefined rules before it is processed or stored.

14. Document data processes:

- Document data processes, including data entry, validation, and transformation steps. This documentation serves as a reference for maintaining consistency and understanding data workflows.

15. Regularly review and update data policies:

- Periodically review and update data policies and procedures to adapt to changing business requirements, technologies, and data quality standards.

16. Regularly monitor and review data:

- Set up regular monitoring processes to review data quality metrics, identify trends, and address any issues promptly. Monitoring helps ensure ongoing data integrity.

By incorporating these best practices into your data management processes, you can establish a strong foundation for maintaining data integrity and reliability. Consistent adherence to these practices helps minimize errors, ensures accurate reporting, and supports informed decision-making.

Chapter 6: Personalized magic: Customizing VBA scripts

The concept of tailoring scripts to individual accounting workflows

Tailoring scripts to individual accounting workflows involves customizing and optimizing automation scripts to align with the specific needs, processes, and requirements of a particular accounting environment. Here's a breakdown of the concept:

1. Understanding individual accounting workflows:

 - Start by gaining a deep understanding of the existing accounting workflows within the organization. Identify key processes, data sources, reporting requirements, and pain points.

2. Identifying repetitive tasks and manual processes:

 - Identify repetitive tasks and manual processes that can be automated to improve efficiency. Look for opportunities to streamline data entry, calculations, report generation, and other routine activities.

3. Defining custom requirements:

 - Work closely with accounting professionals and stakeholders to define custom requirements. Understand the specific data formats, calculations, and reporting formats that are essential for accurate financial reporting.

4. Customizing data input and validation:

- Tailor scripts to handle data input and validation based on the unique requirements of the accounting system. Implement custom validation checks, data cleansing, and transformation processes as needed.

5. Automating data import and integration:

- Customize scripts to automate the import and integration of data from various sources. Ensure seamless data flow between accounting software, external databases, spreadsheets, and other relevant systems.

6. Customizing reporting and analysis:

- Develop scripts that cater to specific reporting and analysis needs. Customize report formats, calculations, and visualization elements to match the preferences of users and stakeholders.

7. Incorporating business rules and logic:

- Embed business rules and logic into scripts to ensure that accounting processes adhere to organizational policies and regulatory requirements. Customize error-checking routines based on specific business rules.

8. User-friendly interfaces:

- Design user-friendly interfaces using VBA UserForms to interact with accounting professionals. Customize input forms, dashboards, and dialog boxes to match the terminology and workflow preferences of users.

9. Role-based automation:

- Implement role-based automation to customize the level of access and functionality available to different users. Tailor scripts to the specific needs of roles such as accountants, financial analysts, or auditors.

10. Scalability and flexibility:

- Design scripts with scalability and flexibility in mind. Ensure that scripts can adapt to changes in data volumes, business processes, and reporting requirements without requiring extensive modifications.

11. Integration with existing systems:

- Tailor scripts to seamlessly integrate with existing accounting systems, ERPs (Enterprise Resource Planning), or other enterprise software solutions. Foster interoperability for a cohesive accounting ecosystem.

12. Compliance with accounting standards:

- Ensure that scripts adhere to accounting standards and regulations applicable to the industry. Customize scripts to generate reports and financial statements that comply with GAAP (Generally Accepted Accounting Principles) or other relevant standards.

13. Custom alerts and notifications:

- Incorporate custom alerts and notifications into scripts to notify users of critical events, errors, or exceptions. Tailor notifications to align with the urgency and significance of specific accounting events.

14. Documentation and training:

- Provide comprehensive documentation for customized scripts. Offer training sessions to accounting professionals to ensure they understand how to use and interact with the tailored automation tools effectively.

15. Regular review and adaptation:

- Regularly review and adapt scripts to evolving accounting workflows. Stay informed about changes in business processes, data sources, and reporting requirements to ensure ongoing relevance and efficiency.

By tailoring scripts to individual accounting workflows, organizations can enhance efficiency, accuracy, and user satisfaction. Customization ensures that automation aligns seamlessly with the unique characteristics and needs of the accounting processes within a specific organization.

Guide on customizing existing scripts for unique needs

Customizing existing VBA scripts for unique needs involves modifying the code to meet specific requirements, workflows, or functionalities that are not addressed by the original script. Here's a guide on how to approach the customization of VBA scripts:

1. Understand the existing script:

   - Before making any changes, thoroughly understand the existing VBA script. Review the code line by line to grasp its structure, functions, and the logic behind each segment.

2. Document requirements:

   - Clearly document the specific requirements and functionalities needed for customization. Identify what aspects of the script need to be modified or enhanced to align with unique needs.

3. Backup the original script:

   - Create a backup copy of the original script before making any changes. This ensures that you can revert to the original version if issues arise during the customization process.

4. Identify customization points:

   - Identify the specific sections or functions within the script that need customization. Look for variables, parameters, or sections where you can introduce modifications without compromising the overall structure.

5. Customize variables and constants:

- If the script uses constants or variables, customize them to reflect unique requirements. Adjust values, ranges, or thresholds based on the specific needs of your application.

6. Modify conditional statements:

- Modify conditional statements (IF, ELSE, etc.) to accommodate additional conditions or change the logic to meet custom requirements. Adjust the flow of the script based on the new conditions.

7. Enhance error handling:

- If the original script lacks robust error handling, enhance it to gracefully handle potential errors specific to your application. Add custom error messages, logging, or actions to be taken in case of errors.

8. Introduce new functions or subroutines:

- If your unique needs require additional functionalities, introduce new functions or subroutines. Keep these modular to maintain a clean and organized script structure.

9. Customize user interfaces:

- If the script involves user interfaces (UserForms), customize them to align with the specific preferences and terminology of users. Enhance the usability and aesthetics of the interfaces.

10. Optimize performance:

- Assess the script's performance and optimize it if needed. Identify areas where efficiency can be improved, such as loop structures, variable usage, or algorithm optimization.

11. Address compatibility issues:

- If the script needs to work with different versions of Excel or other applications, address compatibility issues. Test the script on various platforms to ensure seamless operation.

12. Add comments and documentation:

- As you make changes, add comments and documentation to explain the purpose and functionality of customized sections. This helps future developers or collaborators understand your modifications.

13. Test rigorously:

- Test the customized script thoroughly in a controlled environment. Test different scenarios, edge cases, and user inputs to ensure that the script performs as expected.

14. Gather user feedback:

- If the customization involves user interaction, gather feedback from end-users. Understand how well the customized script meets their needs and make further adjustments based on their input.

15. Iterate and improve:

- Based on testing and feedback, iterate on the customization. Make additional improvements and refinements as needed. Ensure that the final customized script is robust, efficient, and user-friendly.

Remember that customization should be done with care to avoid introducing unintended issues. Regularly communicate with stakeholders and end-users throughout the customization process to align the script with their evolving needs. Customization is an iterative process, and continuous improvement based on user feedback and changing requirements is essential.

Examples of personalized scripts for specialized accounting tasks

Certainly! Below are examples of personalized VBA scripts tailored for specialized accounting tasks. These examples cover common accounting activities such as data validation, report generation, and data analysis. Please note that these are simplified illustrations, and you may need to customize them further to suit your specific requirements.

1. Data validation and formatting:

Objective:

To validate and format data in a specific column, ensuring that it meets certain criteria.

```vba
Sub ValidateAndFormatData()
    Dim dataRange As Range
    Dim cell As Range

    ' Assume data is in column B starting from B2
    Set dataRange = Range("B2:B" & Cells(Rows.Count, "B").End(xlUp).Row)

    For Each cell In dataRange
        ' Check if the data is a valid invoice number (numeric and 6 digits)
        If IsNumeric(cell.Value) And Len(cell.Value) = 6 Then
            ' Format valid invoice numbers
            cell.NumberFormat = "000000"
        Else
            ' Handle invalid invoice numbers
            cell.Interior.Color = RGB(255, 0, 0) ' Mark invalid data with red background
```

```
        Enc If
    Next cell
End Sub
```

2. Automated expense report generation:

Objective:

To automate the generation of monthly expense reports based on a predefined format.

```
Sub GenerateExpenseReport()
    Dim wsSource As Worksheet
    Dim wsReport As Worksheet
    Dim lastRow As Long
    Dim reportRow As Long

    ' Set source and report worksheets
    Set wsSource = Worksheets("Expenses")
    Set wsReport = Worksheets.Add

    ' Copy header from source to report
    wsSource.Rows(1).Copy wsReport.Rows(1)

    ' Find the last row in the source worksheet
    lastRow = wsSource.Cells(wsSource.Rows.Count,
"A").End(xlUp).Row

    ' Initialize reportRow
    reportRow = 2

    ' Loop through each row in the source and copy relevant data
to the report
    For i = 2 To lastRow
```

```
        ' Check if the expense is for the current month (assuming
column B has the date)
        If Month(wsSource.Cells(i, 2).Value) = Month(Date) Then
            ' Copy the entire row to the report
            wsSource.Rows(i).Copy wsReport.Rows(reportRow)
            ' Move to the next row in the report
            reportRow = reportRow + 1
        End If
    Next i
End Sub
```

3. Profit and loss analysis:

Objective:

To analyze profit and loss data and provide a summary report.

```
Sub AnalyzeProfitLoss()
    Dim wsData As Worksheet
    Dim wsSummary As Worksheet
    Dim lastRow As Long
    Dim totalRevenue As Double
    Dim totalExpenses As Double

    ' Set data and summary worksheets
    Set wsData = Worksheets("ProfitLossData")
    Set wsSummary = Worksheets.Add

    ' Copy header from data to summary
    wsData.Rows(1).Copy wsSummary.Rows(1)

    ' Find the last row in the data worksheet
    lastRow = wsData.Cells(wsData.Rows.Count, "A").End(xlUp).Row
```

```vba
    ' Initialize totals
    totalRevenue = 0
    totalExpenses = 0

    ' Loop through each row in the data and calculate totals
    For i = 2 To lastRow
        ' Check if the entry is revenue (assuming column C
indicates revenue)
        If wsData.Cells(i, 3).Value = "Revenue" Then
            totalRevenue = totalRevenue + wsData.Cells(i, 4).Value
        ElseIf wsData.Cells(i, 3).Value = "Expense" Then
            totalExpenses = totalExpenses + wsData.Cells(i,
4).Value
        End If
    Next i

    ' Display the summary in the summary worksheet
    wsSummary.Cells(2, 1).Value = "Total Revenue"
    wsSummary.Cells(2, 2).Value = totalRevenue
    wsSummary.Cells(3, 1).Value = "Total Expenses"
    wsSummary.Cells(3, 2).Value = totalExpenses
    wsSummary.Cells(4, 1).Value = "Net Profit/Loss"
    wsSummary.Cells(4, 2).Formula = "=B2-B3"
End Sub
```

These examples showcase how VBA scripts can be personalized for specific accounting tasks. Depending on your exact requirements and the structure of your data, you may need to make additional customizations to these scripts.

The importance of continuous refinement and adaptation

Continuous refinement and adaptation are essential principles in various aspects of business, technology, and personal development. In the context of processes, strategies, and technologies, these principles play a crucial role in

111

achieving and maintaining optimal performance. Here's why continuous refinement and adaptation are important:

1. Responsive to change:

- In a dynamic and evolving environment, change is inevitable. Continuous refinement allows organizations and individuals to be responsive to changing conditions, whether they are market trends, technological advancements, or shifts in customer preferences.

2. Optimization of processes:

- Regular refinement enables the optimization of processes. By identifying inefficiencies, redundancies, or areas for improvement, organizations can streamline operations, enhance productivity, and reduce costs.

3. Adaptation to new technologies:

- Technology is advancing rapidly, and staying current is crucial for competitiveness. Continuous adaptation allows businesses to embrace and integrate new technologies, ensuring they remain at the forefront of innovation in their industry.

4. Quality improvement:

- Refinement and adaptation contribute to ongoing quality improvement. Whether it's refining product features, service delivery processes, or internal workflows, a commitment to improvement leads to higher-quality outcomes.

5. Risk mitigation:

- Continuous refinement helps identify and address potential risks. By regularly reviewing and adapting strategies, organizations can proactively mitigate risks before they become major issues, enhancing resilience and stability.

6. Enhanced efficiency:

- Refinement leads to increased efficiency. By continuously evaluating and adjusting processes, organizations can eliminate bottlenecks, reduce delays, and ensure that resources are utilized effectively, leading to improved overall efficiency.

7. Customer satisfaction:

- Customer expectations change over time. Continuous adaptation allows businesses to stay aligned with customer needs and preferences, resulting in improved products, services, and overall customer satisfaction.

8. Agility and flexibility:

- In a rapidly changing environment, agility and flexibility are crucial. Continuous refinement ensures that organizations are nimble and can quickly adapt to unforeseen challenges or capitalize on emerging opportunities.

9. Employee engagement:

- Employees are more likely to be engaged and motivated when they see that their work contributes to continuous improvement. Refinement and adaptation foster a culture of learning and growth within the organization.

10. Strategic alignment:

- Regularly refining strategies helps ensure ongoing alignment with organizational goals. It allows for the adjustment of tactics and priorities to stay in line with the broader strategic objectives.

11. Competitive advantage:

- Organizations that continuously refine and adapt have a competitive advantage. They can respond faster to market changes, outpace competitors in innovation, and position themselves as industry leaders.

12. Learning and development:

- Continuous refinement encourages a culture of learning and development. It provides opportunities for individuals and teams to acquire new skills, stay relevant, and contribute to their personal and professional growth.

13. Crisis management:

- When unforeseen challenges or crises arise, organizations that have a culture of continuous refinement are better equipped to navigate uncertainties. They can quickly adjust strategies and operations to manage and mitigate the impact of crises.

14. Sustainability:

- Continuous refinement is essential for long-term sustainability. It allows organizations to adapt to environmental and social changes, comply with evolving regulations, and contribute positively to their communities and the planet.

15. Innovation and creativity:

- Continuous refinement fosters an environment that encourages innovation and creativity. It empowers individuals to experiment with new ideas, take calculated risks, and contribute to the generation of novel solutions.

In summary, continuous refinement and adaptation are not just strategies for survival; they are key drivers of success and resilience. Whether applied to business processes, personal development, or technology integration, these principles enable individuals and organizations to thrive in a rapidly changing world.

Conclusion: Mastering the VBA symphony

The transformative impact of VBA in accounting

The transformative impact of VBA (Visual Basic for Applications) in accounting is profound, ushering in a new era of efficiency, accuracy, and adaptability. Here are key aspects that underline the transformative nature of VBA in the field of accounting:

1. Automation of manual processes:

   - VBA allows accountants to automate manual, repetitive tasks, reducing the time spent on mundane activities such as data entry, formatting, and report generation. This automation enhances productivity and frees up time for strategic analysis.

2. Enhanced accuracy and reduction of errors:

   - By automating calculations and data processing, VBA significantly reduces the risk of human errors. This enhanced accuracy is critical in accounting, where precision is paramount for financial integrity and compliance.

3. Customization for unique accounting workflows:

   - VBA enables the customization of scripts to align with the unique needs of individual accounting workflows. This flexibility ensures that automation solutions are tailored to specific requirements, optimizing efficiency and addressing unique challenges.

4. Streamlined data analysis and reporting:

- VBA empowers accountants to streamline data analysis and reporting processes. Dynamic reports, dashboards, and visualizations can be created, providing real-time insights and facilitating informed decision-making.

5. Integration with external systems:

- VBA facilitates seamless integration with external systems, databases, and APIs. This connectivity ensures a smooth exchange of data between different platforms, eliminating silos and fostering a cohesive accounting ecosystem.

6. Efficient compliance management:

- Automation through VBA eases the burden of compliance management. Accountants can develop scripts to automate regulatory reporting, ensuring timely and accurate submissions while adhering to industry standards and regulations.

7. User-Friendly interfaces and dashboards:

- With the creation of user-friendly interfaces and dashboards using VBA, accountants can interact with data and scripts intuitively. This enhances usability and accessibility, making complex financial information more digestible for end-users.

8. Data security and audit trails:

- VBA allows the implementation of security measures, including access controls and encryption, to protect sensitive financial data. Moreover, the creation of audit trails ensures accountability and transparency, aiding in internal and external audits.

9. Scalability for growing operations:

- As accounting operations expand, VBA solutions remain scalable. Scripts can be adapted and extended to accommodate increased data volumes, new processes, ard the evolving needs of a growing organization.

10. Empowerment for complex calculations:

- VBA empowers accountants to tackle complex financial calculations, enabling the development of sophisticated models for budgeting, forecasting, and scenario analysis. This capability is instrumental in strategic financial planning.

11. Time and resource savings:

- Automat on through VBA results in significant time and resource savings. Accountants can redirect their efforts towards value-added activities, strategic planning, and analysis, fostering a more efficient use of human capital.

12. Adaptability to changing requirements:

- VBA's adaptability allows for continuous refinement and adjustments. Accountants can easily modify scripts to meet changing accounting standards, compliance regulations, or internal processes, ensuring ongoing relevance.

13. Facilitation of innovation:

- VBA encourages innovation by providing a platform for experimenting with new ideas and solutions. Accountants can explore creative ways to address challenges and introduce innovative practices into accounting processes.

14. Creation of learning opportunities:

- The implementation and customization of VBA scripts create learning opportunities for accounting professionals. This fosters a culture of continuous improvement and skill development within the accounting team.

15. Strategic focus and decision support:

- With routine tasks automated, accountants can shift their focus to strategic analysis and decision support. VBA enhances the role of accountants as strategic partners within organizations, contributing to more informed decision-making.

In essence, VBA's transformative impact in accounting lies in its ability to revolutionize traditional processes, drive efficiency, and empower accountants to navigate the complexities of modern financial management with agility and precision. The integration of VBA marks a paradigm shift, positioning accounting practices at the forefront of technological innovation and adaptability.

Why experiment, adapt, and continue VBA journey?

Experimenting, adapting, and continuing the journey with VBA (Visual Basic for Applications) in the realm of accounting and finance offer several compelling reasons for professionals and organizations:

1. Unlocking efficiency gains:

- Through experimentation with VBA, accountants can identify and automate repetitive and time-consuming tasks, unlocking significant efficiency gains. By adapting scripts to streamline processes, professionals can save time and redirect efforts toward more value-added activities.

2. Tailoring solutions to unique needs:

- Experimentation allows for the exploration of VBA's capabilities, enabling professionals to tailor solutions to the unique needs of their accounting workflows. Adapting scripts ensures that automation aligns precisely with specific requirements, optimizing processes for maximum effectiveness.

3. Continuous process improvement:

- The journey with VBA is a continuous cycle of experimentation and adaptation. Regularly reviewing and refining scripts lead to ongoing process improvement This iterative approach ensures that automated solutions evolve to meet changing business requirements and industry standards.

4. Fostering innovation in financial management:

- Experimentation with VBA opens the door to innovation in financial management Professionals can experiment with new ideas, creative solutions, and novel approaches to accounting challenges, pushing the boundaries of what's possible within financial processes.

5. Staying ahead of technological advances:

- The technology landscape is dynamic, and experimentation with VBA keeps professionals ahead of the curve. Adapting to new features, functions, and best practices ensures that accounting processes remain technologically relevant and aligned with industry trends.

6. Addressing evolving compliance requirements:

- Accounting standards and compliance regulations often evolve. Experimenting with VBA enables professionals to address changing compliance requirements by adapting scripts to incorporate new rules and reporting formats, ensuring ongoing adherence.

7. Enhancing data security measures:

- Experimenting with VBA allows for the implementation and adaptation of robust security measures. Professionals can continuously enhance data security by experimenting with encryption methods, access controls, and authentication mechanisms within their scripts.

8. Enabling scalability for business growth:

- Organizations that experiment with and adapt VBA solutions can easily scale their automated processes to accommodate business growth. Adapting scripts to handle increased data volumes and additional complexities ensures that automation remains effective and scalable.

9. Encouraging a culture of learning:

- The VBA journey fosters a culture of continuous learning and development within the accounting team. Experimentation provides opportunities for skill-building, and ongoing adaptation encourages professionals to stay curious and engaged with evolving technologies.

10. Driving strategic decision-making:

- As professionals experiment with VBA to automate routine tasks, they can shift their focus toward strategic decision-making. Adapting scripts to generate more insightful reports and analyses empowers accountants to contribute strategically to organizational goals.

11. Empowering professionals with flexibility:

- Experimentation and adaptation provide professionals with the flexibility to respond to changing business conditions. Whether it's adapting scripts to accommodate new data sources or modifying calculations to align with strategic shifts, VBA offers the agility needed in a dynamic business environment.

12. Optimizing resource utilization:

- By experimenting with VBA to automate tasks, organizations can optimize resource utilization. Adapting scripts ensures that human capital is utilized efficiently, with professionals focusing on tasks that require strategic thinking and nuanced decision-making.

13. Cultivating a proactive mindset:

- The VBA journey encourages a proactive mindset among accounting professionals. Experimenting with automation solutions and adapting them to changing circumstances demonstrates a proactive approach to optimizing processes and embracing technological advancements.

14. Building resilience against challenges:

- Experimentation and adaptation with VBA build resilience against challenges. Professionals can proactively address issues, refine scripts, and ensure that automated processes remain robust and effective even in the face of unforeseen challenges.

15. Contributing to organizational innovation:

- The journey with VBA extends beyond individual tasks to contribute to organizational innovation. Experimenting with new ways to use VBA in financial processes can lead to transformative changes, positioning the organization as an innovator in financial management.

In summary, experimenting, adapting, and continuing the VBA journey in accounting are integral to staying agile, efficient, and technologically relevant. This approach empowers professionals to embrace innovation, optimize processes, and proactively address the evolving landscape of accounting and finance.

Resources for further learning and community engagement

To further your learning in VBA for accounting and finance and engage with the community, consider exploring the following resources:

Online Courses and Tutorials:

1. LinkedIn Learning (formerly Lynda):

- Offers various courses on VBA for Excel and other Microsoft Office applications. Topics range from basics to advanced scripting for financial applications.

2. Udemy:

- Features a wide range of VBA courses tailored for accounting and finance professionals. Look for courses with high ratings and reviews.

3. Coursera:

- Collaborates with top universities and organizations to provide courses on VBA programming. Check for courses related to Excel automation and financial modeling.

4. Codecademy:

- Offers an interactive learning platform with a specific focus on programming languages, including VBA. It's a great resource for hands-on learning.

Books:

1. "Excel VBA Programming For Dummies" by Michael Alexander and John Walkenbach:

- A beginner-friendly guide that covers VBA basics and gradually introduces more advanced concepts, with practical examples.

2. "VBA and Macros for Microsoft Excel" by Bill Jelen and Tracy Syrstad:

- A comprehensive resource for learning VBA and automating tasks in Excel. Suitable for both beginners and intermediate users.

3. "Financial Modeling in Excel For Dummies" by Danielle Stein Fairhurst:

Automate to elevate: VBA secrets for accountants

- Focuses on financial modeling using Excel, including VBA. Provides practical guidance for finance professionals.

4. Series "VBA & macros"

https://www.amazon.com/dp/B0B2L3WH78

Websites anc Forums:

1. https://stackoverflow.com

- A popular Q&A platform where you can find answers to specific VBA questions. Active participation in discussions can enhance your learning.

2. https://www.mrexcel.com/forum/

- Dedicated to Excel and VBA discussions. You can find answers to specific questions, share your knowledge, and learn from others' experiences.

3. https://www.ozgrid.com/forum/):

- An Excel and VBA forum where you can ask questions, share your knowledge, and interact with other Excel enthusiasts.

YouTube Channels:

1. https://www.youtube.com/user/tigermatttube

- Offers a series of video tutorials on Excel VBA for beginners and intermediate users. Covers a variety of topics related to automation and scripting.

2. https://www.youtube.com/user/MyOnlineTrainingHub

- Provides Excel and VBA tutorials, including practical examples and demonstrations for finance and accounting professionals.

Microsoft Documentation:

1. https://docs.microsoft.com/en-us/office/vba/api/overview/excel

- The official documentation provides in-depth information on VBA for Excel. It includes reference materials, guides, and examples.

Community Platforms:

1. https://www.reddit.com/r/excel/

- A community on Reddit dedicated to Excel discussions. You can find threads related to VBA, ask questions, and learn from others' experiences.

2. https://www.mrexcel.com/board/

- The MrExcel forum has a dedicated section for VBA discussions. Engage with the community, share your challenges, and learn from others.

Remember to actively participate in forums, ask questions, and share your experiences. Learning from the community and contributing to discussions is a valuable part of the learning process in programming.